August 2011

Canon and Creed

INTERPRETATION
Resources for the Use of Scripture in the Church

INTERPRETATION

RESOURCES FOR THE USE OF SCRIPTURE IN THE CHURCH

Patrick D. Miller, *Series Editor*
Ellen F. Davis, *Associate Editor*
Richard B. Hays, *Associate Editor*
James L. Mays, *Consulting Editor*

OTHER AVAILABLE BOOKS IN THIS SERIES

Patrick D. Miller, *The Ten Commandments*

ROBERT W. JENSON

Canon and Creed

INTERPRETATION *Resources for the Use of Scripture in the Church*

WESTMINSTER
JOHN KNOX PRESS
LOUISVILLE · KENTUCKY

Book design by Drew Stevens
Cover design by designpointinc.com

Library of Congress Cataloging-in-Publication Data

Jenson, Robert W.
  Canon and creed : interpretation : resources for the use of scripture in the church / Robert W. Jenson.
      p.   cm.—(Interpretation: resources for the use of scripture in the church)
  Includes bibliographical references and index.
  ISBN 978-0-664-23054-8 (alk. paper)
  1. Apostles' Creed. I. Title.
  BT993.3.J46 2010
  238'.11—dc.22

                                                              2010003744

For Pat Miller and Jim Mays,

who first propelled me into writing directly

about the Bible

CONTENTS

SERIES FOREWORD

This series of volumes supplements Interpretation: A Bible Commentary for Teaching and Preaching. The commentary series offers an exposition of the books of the Bible written for those who teach, preach, and study the Bible in the community of faith. This new series is addressed to the same audience and serves a similar purpose, providing additional resources for the interpretation of Scripture, but now dealing with features, themes, and issues significant for the whole rather than with individual books.

The Bible is composed of separate books. Its composition naturally has led its interpreters to address particular books. But there are other ways to approach the interpretation of the Bible that respond to other characteristics and features of the Scriptures. These other entries to the task of interpretation provide contexts, overviews, and perspectives that complement the book-by-book approach and discern dimensions of the Scriptures that the commentary design may not adequately explore.

The Bible as used in the Christian community is not only a collection of books but also itself a book that has a unity and coherence important to its meaning. Some volumes in this new series deal with this canonical wholeness and seek to provide a wider context for the interpretation of individual books as well as a comprehensive theological perspective that reading single books does not provide.

Other volumes in the series examine particular texts, like the Ten Commandments, the Lord's Prayer, and the Sermon on the Mount, texts that have played such an important role in the faith and life of the Christian community that they constitute orienting foci for the understanding and use of Scripture.

A further concern of the series is to consider important and often difficult topics, addressed at many different places in the books of the canon that are of recurrent interest and concern to the church in its dependence on Scripture for faith and life. So the series includes volumes dealing with such topics as eschatology, women, wealth, and violence.

The books of the Bible are constituted from a variety of kinds of literature such as narrative, laws, hymns and prayers, letters, parables, miracle stories, and the like. To recognize and discern the contribution and importance of all these different kinds of material enriches and enlightens the use of Scripture. Volumes in the series provide help in the interpretation of Scripture's literary forms and genres.

The liturgy and practices of the gathered church are anchored in Scripture, as with the sacraments observed and the creeds recited. So another entry to the task of discerning the meaning and significance of biblical texts explored in this series is the relation between the liturgy of the church and the Scriptures.

Finally, there is certain ancient literature, such as the Apocrypha and the noncanonical gospels, that constitutes an important context to the interpretation of Scripture itself. Consequently, this series provides volumes that offer guidance in understanding such writings and explore their significance for the interpretation of the Protestant canon.

The volumes in this second series of Interpretation deal with these important entries into the interpretation of the Bible. Together with the commentaries, they compose a library of resources for those who interpret Scripture as members of the community of faith. Each of them can be used independently for its own significant addition to the resources for the study of Scripture. But all of them intersect the commentaries in various ways and provide an important context for their use. The authors of these volumes are biblical scholars and theologians who are committed to the service of interpreting the Scriptures in and for the church. The editors and authors hope that the addition of this series to the commentaries will provide a major contribution to the vitality and richness of biblical interpretation in the church.

The Editors

ACKNOWLEDGMENTS

I would never have thought of this project without the initiative of two of the series' editors, both of them friends and allies, Patrick Miller and Richard Hays. Blanche Jenson, without whom I cannot imagine my theological life—or any other kind—has played her usual substantive role in the writing of the essay.

Some chapters were tested as the 2009 Burns Lectures at the University of Otago in New Zealand, a flourishing institution whose theological faculty I must thank for a large, learned, and persistent group of participating students, teachers, and clergy, and for splendid care and feeding of the visiting lecturer and his wife. At Otago we found old friends and made new ones.

Introduction

Why did the editors of this series include a study of *Canon and Creed*? I undertook the assignment because I trust these particular editors' judgment and because I found the implied questions intriguing. But in thinking this matter vital, editors and author may alike be idiosyncratic. One may safely suppose that neither canon or creed, nor yet their relation, is high on many contemporary believers' list of concerns. There are—or so it has for some time generally been thought—weightier matters to worry us: at the particular moment of this writing, perhaps "the environment" or "sexuality."

Who lies awake over the relation of canon and creed, when pieces of one's church are threatening to depart, into witness for the true faith or into schism, according to viewpoint? Or when a church's demographics portend extinction, or at least further job cuts at headquarters? If the churchly commissions that pronounce about "sexuality" or "peace" or similar matters remember that they are supposed to consult the Bible and the church's doctrine, and call in the certified experts on each, the report of the experts is regularly that their disciplines offer no great help with the particular problem—and if they do offer something and it appears in the report, it will be acknowledged in the introduction but its influence will not be prominent in the proposals.

At this ecumenically untoward moment, there are even renewed concerns about confessional identity. Since the creed and the

1

Scriptures are shared by most of the separated churches, it is unlikely that they will greatly help, for example, the Lutherans discover why they are not Methodists. Scripture and creed are ecumenical possessions, and the churches are at the moment not very interested in the ecumene. Even the officially and thereby in its case permanently committed Roman Catholic Church currently manifests little actual interest in ecumenism at national or diocesan levels. And the mantra among Protestants is "What is the special contribution of our denomination?" "Contribution" sounds ecumenical, but one need not be overly cynical to suspect that the question actually seeks reasons for maintaining denominational distinctives. Neither canon nor creed will provide such reasons; indeed, the most that could be expected from either would be condemnation of the question.

In some academic and ecclesial circles, canon and creed are even assumed to be in competition for our loyalty. The Scripture is regarded as a deposit of ancient Israelite and early Christian "religion"; and the creeds are thought to be the result of later and alienating "philosophical" influences. Harnack's dictum that creedal doctrine is the result of the "hellenization of the gospel," the latter to be found in a historical-critically edited New Testament, has been often and conclusively debunked, but continues to inhibit many scholarly consciences. Thus it is widely supposed that we can cling to Scripture or cling to church doctrine, or possibly to both in different contexts, but cannot cling to both with the same grasp. The biblical-studies establishment still greets proposals to read Scripture by the light of the creed with great suspicion, or indeed occasional outrage. And a proposal that the creed might be read by the light of Scripture may be met with mere wonderment at how the varied ancient documents collected as Scripture are supposed to help in the alien realm of currently effective church doctrine.

Perhaps contemporary bewilderment by canon and creed is itself among the reasons why the editors conceived this project. The problem of reception that the author foresees may be the very problem they hope renewed attention will ameliorate.

It may even be that it is precisely because the mutuality of canon and creed has slipped from our grasp that so many other aspects of the church's life do the same. For canon and creed appeared in the church's history as—or so the church has believed—Spirit-given reminders of what sort of community the church must be if it is indeed to be church; thus alienation from the mutual import of canon and creed may be occasioned by, and in turn occasion, alienation from the church's reason for existence. If we cannot say what it means for the affairs of the church that we have these particular Scriptures, or what convictions center and delimit the life of the church, or how our Scripture and our convictions work together, how do we make an identifiable community?

Any community that intends to live for more than a moment, that hopes to remain itself through some term of yesterday-today-and-tomorrow, will have to deal with the fragility of an identity thus stretched across time. Many communities, to be sure, are unconcerned about their temporal self-identity, or make some effort to attend to it but fail without much regret; thus a social club may have occasional discussions of its original high-minded "mission" but not be overly alarmed when little comes of them. The church's diachronic identity is as threatened by the passage of time as is that of any other community, and unlike some other communities, it cannot be relaxed about the threat. It is always a real and vital question: Is the so-called church of today indeed the same community as the church of the apostles? Which is to say, as the church of Christ? To be sure, we are permitted to believe that the gates of hell will not finally prevail against the universal church, but there is no such guarantee for the Presbyterians or the Baptists, as there was none for the great churches of Pergamum or Hippo, now vanished without trace.

The structure of a community's self-identity through time depends on what sort of community it is, and so then does the nature of possible threats to that identity. What sort of community is the church? Perhaps we may find ecumenical agreement in a truly minimal proposition: the church is the community of a *message*, that the God of Israel has raised his servant Jesus from the dead. Anyone who cannot agree even to so much belongs to a different religious community than do the author and initially intended readers of this book—though of course all are welcome to eavesdrop and even intrude on the conversation.

Samuel is to tell Jane that the Lord has raised Jesus, and do so in such a fashion as to make the import of this comprehensible for Jane; and if Jane believes it, she is to tell Wu in similar fashion; and so on. Thus the message is carried on and thus also arises the community of Samuel and Jane and Wu and so on, which we call the church. Time's particular threat to such a community will be obvious to anyone who has played the game sometimes called "telephone": a circle is formed, the leader quietly speaks a phrase or two to the one on her right, and he to the one on his right, and so around to the beginning, whereupon it is regularly found that the process of tradition has disintegrated the message—often hilariously, which is the point of the game.

In the case of the church, the threat is made especially severe by the need repeatedly so to shape the message as to make it comprehensible for new sorts of hearers, by the need not merely to recite the gospel but to interpret it as its messengers enter new cultural or historical situations. What, for instance, can ". . . raised . . . from the dead" mean in, as we are constantly told, a "scientific" age? And if a drift or indeterminacy of the message encountering some new consensus of the world's opinion does not prompt us to watchfulness, if we can greet every accommodation to the common wisdom of some time or place as doubtlessly necessary to be "relevant" or "inclusive" or whatever, our complacency is but another and indeed chief manifestation of what ails us.

Through the church's first century or so, dangers to the sheer diachronic self-identity of the message and the community were not felt as such, though problems and controversies enough plagued the congregations, some of which we in retrospect may think did in fact threaten the church's identity. Apostles or apostles' disciples or colleagues of apostles' disciples were experienced as a presence in the integral community of the church, which thus had a living memory of Jesus' words and works and of the witness to his resurrection. The church simply knew at a communal first hand what the message was. But two things happened around the middle of the second century.

First, as one would expect by that time, the telephone-game problem became apparent. A living memory of the Lord could no longer be so immediately dispositive. How do we know what does or does not belong to the message? How do we know if we heard rightly from our predecessors? How do we find the direction and limits of newly possible or demanded interpretation? Certainty about such matters was no longer so unquestionably present in the church's self-consciousness as it once had been.

4

Moreover, this in any case inevitable development had a particularly dangerous context in what has been called "the gnostic crisis" of the second century: a proliferation of claims, arising from the religiously unhinged culture of late Mediterranean antiquity, to have been entrusted with the "real" message and significance of Jesus. Whether there was a single movement to be called "gnos-tic*ism*" is disputed and need not concern us. Is Jesus a human person, who was born of a human mother, who had a human career as itinerant prophet and rabbi, who was executed by human authorities for his presumptions, who was then raised from death by the God he addressed as "Father," and who precisely so is the Son of that Father, as the church of the Gospel writers or of such second-century teachers as Ignatius of Antioch or Justin the Martyr believed? Or was the true saving reality an emanation from a previously unknown spiritual world, that temporarily inhabited the human Jesus in order to communicate secret and salvific knowledge of that other reality, and that did not itself die or then need to be raised, but simply returned to its own place? As the various "gnostic" theologians and mystagogues more or less agreed? It soon became apparent to teachers of the nascent catholic church that their own teaching and that of the thinkers and would-be reformers we label "gnostic" could not both be true.

Second, a palpable stretch of time had now gone by, and the Lord had not so quickly returned in glory as had seemingly been promised (e.g., see Mark 9:1). Unexpectedly, the church found itself with a past history, and so—if the delay did not simply disprove the message—had to anticipate a future history also, in which institutions of historical continuity would be needed.

At this juncture, the Spirit—or so again most of the ecumene has believed—granted touchstones of the true gospel and just so institutions of the community's historical self-identity. Three linked developments are commonly noted: the formation of a specifically Christian scriptural canon of Old and New Testaments, increased attention to explicit statements of the faith, and the appearance of a sacramentally ordered church governance with special responsibility for continuity of teaching and life: the episcopate. Two of these are our assignment.

It is doubtless a sign of the Reformation milieu of press, editors and author that the third institution is not assigned. We may be grateful for the omission, since discussing and relating all three in their complicated linkages would be a much more daunting and even treacherous task, both for me and for readers. Even so, I have found myself compelled to stretch a point and devote a short chapter to the emergence and role of episcopal governance. Moreover, readers should be aware of a certain still remaining disembodiment, a concentration on texts detached from their interweaving with the church's personally embodied continuity. The late second-century bishop and theologian Irenaeus of Lyon—whom I, like everyone else who writes on these matters, will repeatedly cite—could not summon canon and creed against the heretics without simultaneously claiming that "we can name those whom the apostles made bishops in the churches, and their successors up to ourselves" (Irenaeus, *Against Heresies* 3.3.1).

A first part of the following will be devoted to the basic questions. An initial chapter will consider the notions of canon and creed for themselves. I will not offer antecedent "definitions of terms"; launching an even partially historical inquiry in that way is generally unwise, for it is by the generosity of its references that ordinary language has purchase on the messy history we in fact inhabit. The true import even of such—to be sure, modestly—technical terms as appear in our title emerge only as we actually use them to investigate the matters to which they point. We do of course need to know in a preliminary way where to look for this matter; if "canon" and "creed" do not point to, say, military exercises, to what *do* they point?

The second chapter will take up the place and role of the Old Testament, as it is canon for the church. It is sometimes asked, "How did the church come to adopt Israel's Scripture?" We will see that this is a wrong question; the right question reads the other way around: "How did and does Israel's Scripture accommodate the church? If at all?"

A third chapter will then seek to clarify, historically and conceptually, the relation between the Old Testament canon and the developing creedal tradition. The "rule of faith" repelled gnostic and other attacks on the place of the Old Testament. What effect did that have on both? If any?

The fourth and fifth chapters will cover much the same ground as the second and third, but now with respect to the New Testament. We will find that the relations are, however, quite different, and the division of labor between the two chapters will shift accordingly. The Old Testament was always there, but the notion and fact

6

of a New Testament canon developed in overlap with the notion and fact of the creed.

Part 2 will bring what I will call "extensions" of the central assignment. Chapter 6, the first in this part, will extend the concern for canon by considering the place of "the canonical text" over against reconstructions of what I will call "ancestor texts"; it will also consider the vexed question of which version of the Old Testament is the church's canonical Scripture. Chapter 7 extends our concern for the creedal tradition, by analyzing the role of authoritative doctrine developed after the time of creed-making; such doctrine is here labeled "dogma." And Chapter 8 is where I will insert a brief descriptive discussion of episcopacy.

A third and final part of the work will bear the title "Creed/ Dogma and Scriptural Exegesis" and will try to provide some proof of the antecedent pudding, or at least of a portion of it. An initial chapter, number 9 of the work, will propose that the creed may be regarded and wielded as the "critical theory" appropriate to the reading of Scripture. Two following chapters will seek to demonstrate this proposal on texts, one from each Testament. And chapter 12 will attempt a somewhat similar exemplification for dogma and a text of Scripture.

In obedience to an editorial mandate not to clutter the pages with references and to use no footnotes at all, I will—with considerable relief—give little indication of how I have come by much of the information presented or relied upon. Readers will have to trust some decades of intermittently relevant reading and reflection. In the discussion of canon, readers will notice relatively frequent reference to Campenhausen's monumental work (*Entstehung*). I rely on his exhaustive researches as does everybody concerned with the canon, even if later scholars, including myself, question some of his conclusions. In discussion of creed, readers will note a similar though more limited reliance on J. N. D. Kelly (*Creeds*). So far as I know, the interpretations and relations suggested are my own except where dependence is noted.

PART ONE

The Central Concerns

CHAPTER 1

"Canon" and "Creed"

As promised in the introduction, I will begin by considering these notions for their own sake. As also promised, I will refrain from prior definitions. Indeed, the bulk of this chapter will be historical, since clarifying and relating the notions of canon and creed, as these actually appear and function in the church's discourse, is inseparable from reviewing certain aspects of the actual development of the Christian canon and the Christian creed; that is to say, of the phenomena to which these terms point.

We will first consider canon. In recent discussion, two construals of the phrase "canon of Christian Scripture" have competed, and it may be that a third has just entered the arena. The overt argument between the two has been about the time at which the church can be said to have such a thing (compendiously to the arguments: Allert, *High View?* 102–8). It might therefore seem that for our purposes we could ignore the dispute, but the historiographic difference and a conceptual difference condition one another. We should note also that the canon whose emergence is in question is the full canon of Old *and* New Testaments, since the Old Testament was there from the church's beginning.

Some hold that the church can be said to have its canon of Scripture when an identifiable and substantial set of the writings that will make up our New Testament is regularly cited as authoritative for the church's teaching and practice and is made equal to

11

Old Testament Scripture in that role. On this construal, the canon of Scripture was functional in the latter part of the second century, for churchly writers of the time refer to and in that fashion cite a limited set of writings, roughly those that now make our New Testament, and conduct arguments for or against the propriety of admitting particular writings to this role. Irenaeus, writing around 180, is always instanced: thus early in his work *Against Heresies*, he puts "the Lord's parables . . . and the apostles' words" in a single set with "the prophets' sayings"—all of these *partes pro toto*—as indispensable witnesses to the faith and as the sacred texts that heretics profane (1.8.1).

Those who argue for a second-century canon are undeterred by remaining vagueness at its margins: "That the compass of neither the Christian nor the Jewish canons was fully fixed, did not damage their authority" (Campenhausen, *Entstehung*, 7). A canon with fuzzy edges, it is maintained, can be authoritative Scripture as well as one with absolutely set edges. The fact that Judaism's authorities had not yet formally delineated their Scripture when it funded the church's beginning made no difference for this Scripture's authority either in Judaism or for the nascent church. Nor was the late second-century New Testament precisely delineated, which again did not prevent it from being Scripture. For those who take this point of view, the question of when the Christian canon was "closed" is therefore of little theological import.

Others contend that since a "canon"—a rule—of Scripture must be both Scripture itself as a criterion of the church's life, and a criterion of what is in fact to be regarded as Scripture, there is no canon until lists of included writings or formally stated criteria of inclusion appear and are widely accepted. Such things do not certainly emerge until the fourth century, although what may have been an approach to such a list appears in an apparently earlier text, partially preserved in an itself fragmentary manuscript called the "Muratorian fragment" (on this document see Campenhausen, *Entstehung*, 282–93; Hahneman, *Muratorian Fragment*). For those who take this view of the matter, the question of datable closings of the Jewish and Christian canons assumes greater importance.

And then there is the aforementioned recent hypothesis, that seems to be an improved version of one much earlier advanced by Harnack (*Entstehung*, 47–48). It is impossible not at least to note the proposal that what happened in the later second century was

12

not an informal coalescence in churchly use of writings regarded as scriptural, but the commercial production and sale of a book, a uniformly edited anthology to which the publisher gave the title "The New Testament." This edition is then supposed to have become the model for the text and structure found in the most important surviving early manuscripts, and may therefore be called the "canonical edition" (Trobisch, *First Edition*).

I cannot here evaluate or even describe the complex arguments that support this hypothesis: they needed a long book to develop and do not lend themselves to a summary. But if such an event occurred, it is not clear that this makes much difference for our present purposes. If a Christian publisher of the later second century—and there surely may have been such enterprises—brought out a collection of Gospels, Pauline letters, and other writings, it will have been because these were the texts that Christian congregations, and individual Christians with the money to buy expensive hand-produced books, already wanted to have at hand. Thus, for our purposes, the proposal seems to rejoin the first of the options already described.

Whichever of the two construals may be more appropriate for other theological or scholarly purposes, we must here adopt the first. For it is the structure and rationale of Scripture itself that must be our concern in investigating its relation to the creedal tradition. To construe "canon" in such fashion as to refuse its application before the late third century would abstract from the decisive history both of the actual canon and of the actual creeds and reduce our task to sheer conceptual analysis, a proceeding inappropriate to the topic. This also means that I will not in this essay pursue the question of when or how the canon was closed.

It thus turns out that in trying to locate what "canon" points to, what we actually need to specify is "Scripture." What do we mean by so labeling a body of literature? As it happens, we can be more definitionally apodictic about "scripture" than about "canon" itself.

Most developed religious communities have a body of texts that, in the language of Western scholarship, we are likely to call their "scripture." A preliminary characterization of scripture will therefore belong more to the phenomenology of religions than to Christian theology more properly considered. Let me propose: a religious community's scripture is a body of literature that is fixed in some medium that preserves it—which may simply be trained

13

memories—and that precisely in that fixity is necessary for the per-durance of the community.

The mode of this necessity varies greatly, according to the nature of the community in question. Thus, for an extreme instance, the Vedas consist mostly of hymns and rubrics for rites that have not actually been performed for more than a millennium; their rubrics may be chanted but are not followed. Thus it is not what outsiders might consider the Vedas's content or purpose that is necessary for Brahmanism; it is rather their sheer existence as links to the Aryan beginning. For an oppositely extreme instance, the textual collec-tion we call the New Testament is necessary for the perdurance of the church only at one remove: it provides a norm for the message on the authenticity of which the perdurance of the church does indeed depend—"the gospel"—a message that is itself primally ver-bal and linguistically fluid. Indeed, the church perdured without a New Testament for more than a century.

It may therefore be already apparent that the Old Testament and the New Testament are Scripture for the church in different ways. The Old Testament was Scripture for the apostles and other disciples before they were apostles and disciples. The language that speaks about the church "adopting" or "taking over" the Jewish canon is malaprop, however eminent some may be who fall into it—as even Campenhausen occasionally does (e.g., *Entstehung*, 5). The New Testament, on an exactly other hand, is a product of the church, and at a particular juncture of its history. If the Lord had returned as quickly as was first expected, the church would never have depended or been thought to depend on Scripture other than Israel's. We will encounter this difference and its implications throughout this study.

"Creed" is a less universal religious phenomenon. If we take the Apostles' Creed as a paradigm, Buddhism, for example, has nothing remotely like it. Indeed, one scholar of Christianity's creedal devel-opment says bluntly that "Christianity is the only major religion to set such store by creeds" (Young, *Creeds*, 1). Christians and West-ern scholars are likely to refer to "the creed" of another religion when they perceive in its life a text or set of recurring affirmations that seem to be a functional or formal analogue to the Apostles' Creed or Nicene Creed, even though the devotees of most other religions do not themselves think in categories appropriate to what Christians know as creeds.

14

In the context of my assignment, we cannot restrict ourselves to formulas of the exact type we are now most likely to call "creeds," for this again would too much abstract from the actual history. In this study "creed" will cover not only the relatively fixed catechetical-baptismal confessions usually now so labeled, but also and foundationally the "rule of faith" to which the church appealed before it had fixed creeds and for some time after the latter began to take shape.

The rule of faith, the *regula fidei*, was a sort of communal linguistic awareness of the faith delivered to the apostles, which sufficed the church for generations. This gift of the Spirit guided missionary proclamation, shaped instruction, identified heresy, and in general functioned wherever in the church's life a brief statement of the gospel's content was needed.

We speak of "the" rule of faith, though there was no one text in general use, and indeed strictly speaking no *text* at all. The *regula fidei*, though directed and attuned to statement in language, was not itself written or even memorized; the phrase "communal linguistic awareness" in the previous paragraph was carefully chosen. The early pastors and theologians who invoked the rule of faith in their teaching, liturgical instructions, or polemics lived in a community experienced as immediately identical with that of the Lord's first witnesses, a community that was for them a single living reality embracing the Lord, his immediate witnesses, and themselves. Thus they located the "rule" of this community's faith in its communal self-consciousness. In this matter also we may hear the regularly archetypical Irenaeus of Lyon: the church, though scattered throughout the world and correspondingly diverse, "believes these things as if she had but one soul and one and the same heart" (*Against Heresies* 1.10.1). As we will repeatedly note in the following chapters, and indeed in the next paragraph, this confidence in the community's communal consciousness is in fact a confidence in the guiding presence of the Spirit.

Thus the self-identity of the rule in its various formulations was constituted by the community's inner fidelity to itself. Irenaeus again: the church as a living community is "as it were, a vessel" into which the apostles had poured "everything that pertains to truth" (*Against Heresies* 3.4.1). When the early pastors and theologians adduced the rule, they could be very free in stating it and yet be confident that the momentarily appropriate formulation expressed

15

the very same rule as other and perhaps verbally quite different formulations. For they drew from the cistern of truth itself, the community of which they themselves were members and teachers. This confidence in the community's truth is again a confidence in the Spirit.

The *regula fidei* can perhaps be discerned already in New Testament documents, though we will not here go very far into the question. Paul's specification of prophecy that is done *kata tēn analogian tēs pisteōs*, "according to the analogy of the faith" (Rom. 12:6, my trans.), may refer to something like what would later be called the *regula* of faith—and then again it may not. Cullmann provides perhaps overgenerous lists of passages that may show its presence, and of contexts in which these formulations may have been used: baptism, common worship, exorcism, persecution, and polemics (*Confessions*, 19–34).

Baptism had a more specific structure than the other contexts in which a rule for believing was needed, and baptismal confession quickly assumed a relatively fixed form. When admitting to participation in the Eucharist by baptism, God and the church needed to ask whether a candidate had grasped what he or she was taking on. And so, as the candidate took the morally revolutionary and quite possibly fatal step, the candidate would be asked, "Do you believe in God the Father? The one who . . . ?" "Do you believe in the Son? The one who . . . ?" "Do you believe in the Spirit? The one who . . . ?" For centuries, the recitals marked above by ellipses varied from church to church. But the basic triadic structure was given by the nature of the event: the church knew itself instructed by the Lord to initiate new believers "in the name of the Father and of the Son and of the Holy Spirit" (Matt. 28:19).

Whether there was a time before the trinitarian mandate attested in Matthew became a general rule, during which baptisms were sometimes conducted solely in the name of Christ, is disputed and likely to remain so. Such passages as the Acts description of the baptism of Cornelius and his family (Acts 10:48) are in any case not to the point (contra Cullmann, *Confessions*), since any historically conceivable act of baptism can be described as done "in the name of Jesus Christ," regardless of the naming formula used.

16 The boundary between the variously statable *regula fidei* and relatively formalized baptismal confessions was doubtless not so clear as the foregoing might suggest. The evidence does not permit

firm conclusions about how baptismal practice influenced the content of the rule of faith, but such practice was certainly part of the communal consciousness that the rule brought to speech. In the other direction, the rule of faith surely controlled the recitals that followed "in the Father . . ." and "in the Son . . ." and "in the Holy Spirit . . . ," though again we cannot recover the history in detail. Some of the earliest expressions of the rule of faith are christological recitals (texts in Young, *Creeds*, 7–9; proposed reconstruction of the history in Cullmann, *Confessions*, 38–42) much like those that appear in the second article of the recorded baptismal creeds; here we perhaps can think of quite direct dependence.

Longer and explicitly so-labeled statements of the rule of faith, in such second- and third-century writers as Irenaeus, Tertullian, Cyprian, and Novatian (texts in Schaff, *Creeds*, 2:12–21) are often formally trinitarian in structure, but tend also to include theologoumena that would hardly have been included in a neophyte's baptismal confession. Thus one of Irenaeus's versions of the rule reads, "The church . . . received from the apostles and their disciples the faith in one God the Father Almighty, the Creator of heaven and earth, . . . and in the one Jesus Christ, the Son of God, who was incarnate for our salvation; and in the Holy Spirit, who through the prophets preached the economies," but then runs off into an account of the christological "economy" that amounts to a short dogmatic treatise on "incarnate" (*Against Heresies* 1.10.1).

Late in the third century and through the fourth century, creeds appear that are connected with baptism but not formulated as interrogations (to this and the following, Kelly, *Creeds*, 30–52). These seem to have developed in the period's firmly structured catechumenate, in the intensive instruction and discipline then demanded as preparation for baptism. As summaries of the faith about which the candidates would be questioned during baptism, they were patterned on the triune baptismal questioning and the recitals there attached to the three interior names. In accord with the spiritual and not merely intellectual character of the catechumenate, the imparting of this creed and its recitation by the candidate at the conclusion of his or her preparation were solemn acts. Somewhere in the East there was a fully developed and formulated such creed by 325 at the latest, since the Council of Nicaea appropriated and interpolated it—for quite nonbaptismal purposes, about which more later.

17

Thus, in the initiation orders of this period, the candidate confessed twice: once to prove her readiness by reciting a creed at the last moment of preparation, and in baptism itself by responding affirmatively to the questions on which that recitation had been patterned. With the decline of the catechumenate, confession of the catechetical creed migrated to be part of baptism itself, and then it assumed the place of baptismal confession, becoming the baptismal creed to which we are accustomed. And from this location, a local creed approved by the bishop for baptism "must quickly have ousted all other summaries of belief current in the district" (Kelly, *Creeds*, 101), to become something like a textually fixed *regula fidei*. The two such creeds that history has given general currency—the Nicene-Constantinopolitan Creed and the Apostles' Creed—now hold that place for the universal church.

Finally in this chapter, it will perhaps already be apparent that the function of neither "canon"/"Scripture" nor "creed" can be grasped without reference to the other—which makes the theme of this book. Their alienation from one another in some modern scholarship and in the consciousness of some parts of the church is, ironically, blatantly ahistorical.

CHAPTER 2

Israel's Scripture

What shall we call this body of literature in its role as Christian canon? The question is not insignificant.

Rabbinic Judaism regularly calls it the "Tanakh," the acronym of a Hebrew list of the Scripture's main divisions, which in English are "The Torah, the Prophets, and the [other] Writings." This is a straightforward device, but it would be a little late and more than a little intrusive for Christians now to adopt it. Lately it has become fashionable for Christians to speak of "The Hebrew Scriptures." But this is an empty recourse since the phrase has no import in either rabbinic Judaism or the church. For Judaism "Hebrew Scriptures" is redundant; whereas the church has always regarded Scripture as inherently translatable, and for centuries it read the Greek version called the Septuagint as its Old Testament, and in the West it read the Latin Vulgate for yet further centuries as the authoritative text—which does not mean that scholars did not also check with the Hebrew if they could.

In this essay we will abide by the church's tradition and speak of "the Old Testament." The fashion for "Hebrew Scriptures" results mostly from supposing that the adjective "old" must be offensive to Jews and thus from looking for a blandly descriptive label. The offense, however, is probably more to Christians' own bad conscience about "supersessionism," the usual label for an opinion formerly general in the church that Christianity had succeeded old Israel in such fashion as to leave no role for any other succession, that is, for continuing Judaism. When in the following I speak of the "Old Testament," it is with the stipulation that "old" is to mean simply "older" or even "senior," and not "antiquated" or "superseded."

What then is the Old Testament's necessity for the church, such that it is a canon of Scripture for Christians? We have already noted it in the previous chapter: the Old Testament's simple and thus absolute priority. The Old Testament and its status as Scripture were and are just *there* for the church, as a fact antecedent to its existence and foundational for its self-understanding. For the church the Old Testament is canon as a sheer given, underivable from other facts or axioms. Therefore I have from the start rejected a supposition hidden in the way the matter is often stated, in both scholarly and churchly everyday discourse: as if the church somehow "took over" or "accepted" old Israel's Scripture. On the contrary, Israel's Scripture accepted—or did not accept—the church.

The church initially could not ask and still should not ask: "Why should/did we adopt Israel's Scripture?" "What do we need it for?" The Law, the Prophets, and the Writings were Scripture for those who first believed the resurrection, and in that role they were antecedent to and indeed independent of this new conviction. The real question was and is this: "Can Israel's Scripture accept this proclamation of Jesus' resurrection and this new movement within Israel?" "Why does Israel's Scripture need Jesus and his disciples?" And that question is real. The rabbis gathered in council after the temple's last destruction asked it and answered: the Torah does not support this message, and the last thing that yet again distressed and dispersed Israel needs is this new sect, which does not uniformly keep the law and may even be heretical with respect to the singleness of God.

In the initial church, even the real question could not be directly posed. For God had answered it before the church could ask it, by the very occasion and content of the church's faith, the resurrection itself. However reserved Jesus may or may not have been about applying specific messianic titles to himself, his preaching and actions manifestly claimed that he and his community were uniquely and exactly what Israel according to its Scripture needed; and when he was executed on account of this claim, the God of Israel confirmed it by raising him up.

20

Nevertheless, the pressure of the directly unaskable question appears throughout the discourse of the primal church, which regularly dealt with arguable or puzzling matters by linking them to some feature of Israel's Scripture. And for a hundred years or more it was always the new gospel that was justified by Israel's Scripture, never the other way around (Campenhausen, *Entstehung*, 68). Even Paul's tortured reasonings about the Old Testament law did not defend the law, that also for him needed no defending; even at Romans 7:7–13 he defends not the law itself but a judgment about the law that could be attributed to him. Rather, Paul defended the gospel's openness to Gentiles as Gentiles, against the threat to their inclusion that the law seemed to pose, and defended himself against suspicion that he evaded the threat by mitigating the divine authority of the law. Moreover, Paul conducted this defense strictly by scholarly exegesis of the Old Testament, however strange some of his methods may seem to modern Gentiles.

Among the early gospel tradition's recourses to the Old Testament, perhaps the most striking is its account of the crucifixion. Jesus' execution was a problem for the earliest believers: How could the Messiah have been put to death? Why could he not simply have entered into his kingdom? Why had he not gone straight to his glorification, without the detour through death? We late-coming believers tend not to be puzzled by Jesus' crucifixion since we think of the inherited explanations before we think of the event itself. But the little gathering in Jerusalem, even after the resurrection, did not understand and needed to. And they came to understand by reciting an account of the crucifixion in which every detail somehow ties the event to the Old Testament (some detail in Jenson, *Theology*, 1:182–85). This is not done on a deliberate scheme of prophecy and fulfillment, nor is it figural interpretation of the Old Testament passages; it is simply a display of narrative harmony between the old history and texts and the unexpected and terrible event. As for something more like a *doctrine* of the crucifixion, it is only a slight exaggeration to say that in the New Testament Isaiah 53 and certain psalms just *are* that doctrine.

We must therefore be careful in stipulating the difference that the crucifixion and resurrection made for the role of the Old Testament. In the New Testament itself, the Old Testament's theological authority is unaffected. The Old Testament's identification of the Lord as "the one who rescued Israel from Egypt" is indeed

21

completed by "the one who rescued the Lord Jesus from death";
but it is not replaced (Soulen, *God*); and in general the New Testament simply assumes the whole of Israel's story about God's works
with his people. Whatever problems the Old Testament law made
for a soon predominantly Gentile church, Jesus' own remembered
words confirmed that the law reveals God's will. And Israel's prophets were the very teachers from whom the primal church learned
why Jesus is needed.

Even phenomena such as Jesus' saying, with reference to the
Old Testament, "It was said of old . . . , but I say . . . ," (e.g., Matt.
5:31–32), do not make such a break with Old Testament Scripture
as might be thought. Indeed, such freedom was not unheard of also
in Judaism; for a striking instance, some of the old rabbis taught
that Moses had truly brought from God the "severe decree" that
the sins of the fathers would be visited on the children "unto the
third and fourth generation" (Exod. 20:5 KJV), but that then "along
came Ezekiel" and, as recorded at Ezekiel 18:20, revoked it (Levey,
Targum, 59).

Undoubtedly it makes a decisive difference that "the old Scripture is now directed to Christ" (Campenhausen, *Entstehung*, 5). But
imprecise talk of the novelty and absoluteness of the revelation in
Christ can easily lead us astray. The emphasis—perhaps especially
found in Reformation theology—on the unique fullness of the revelation in Christ can be maintained only if it is also taught, with the
ancient church, that when God revealed himself to old Israel's law-
givers, prophets, and sages, it was "in the person" of that same Christ
that he was present to them. The indeed singular revelation in Christ
includes his presence in the Old Testament: the Word that "was in the
beginning" and is incarnate as Jesus (John 1:1–14) is the very Word
that "came to" the prophets (e.g., Ezek. 1:3), is offered back to God
in the Psalms, and moves Israel's history (Isa. 55:11). If Christ interpreted the old Scripture "with authority," as if he were the author, it
was because, in the final ontological analysis, that is what he is.

So what did and should it mean for the role of the Old Testament in the church, that in some new way it is now "directed
to Christ"? We see that our question must be limited: we cannot
ask *why* the Old Testament is Scripture after Christ's resurrection,
but only about the *way* in which the Old Testament canon actually functions within the risen Christ's community. And to the latter
question there is a reasonably clear answer: from the beginning the

church has read the Old Testament as *narrative* of God's history with his people, the people that is now in mission as the church—which of course is not to suggest that the Fathers or medievals were "narrative theologians."

The church read and reads the Old Testament in this way because the church's gospel is itself a narrative, even in its briefest statements, and because this gospel story identifies itself as the climax and content of a narrative told by the Old Testament. As to what in turn maintained the church's grasp of the narrative character of the gospel itself, against powerful temptation to turn it into moral or religious instruction, it was the rule of faith that did this, for the rule in all its versions simply listed a set of events and specified their agent. In the integral continuity of the initial church's self-consciousness, what she most simply and immediately knew was the plotted sequence of God's acts that Irenaeus called "the economy."

Here again we must be careful. The temptation to regard the Old Testament as surpassed can easily recur at just this point, and indeed has. The neo-Protestant theology of the nineteenth and twentieth centuries, that spoke so much about "history," often used its invocation of history to relativize the authority of the Old Testament. That the gospel identifies itself as the culmination and content of the Old Testament's story can be made to mean that the Old Testament now serves to provide historical background for the gospel. On this construal, we do need the Old Testament to understand the New, but it is only in the New that we find the message itself. Ascertaining and circulating the needed background information can then be left to interested scholars.

On the contrary, the history of God with his people, indeed both centered and encompassed in Christ, is precisely as a *whole* God's self-revelation. Why, for a central instance, can Christians pray the Psalms? According to the ancient church, it is because it was always the Messiah at the head of his people who prayed them; in Augustine's fine phrase, it was always "the total Christ," the *totus Christus*, Christ as the head and his folk as the body, who gathered in the temple with these hymns and lamentations.

We perhaps may better understand the particular nature of the church's obedience to the Old Testament, both conceptually and historically, if we compare it to that of rabbinic Judaism. When Judaism and the church read the Tanakh/Old Testament, their ways sometimes simultaneously part and converge: they read

23

differently but can nevertheless read together, an experience that has appeared at various times in their histories and is now again emerging. To understand why this can happen, we must remember that *neither* community was a direct historical continuation of the Israel that came to an end with the last destruction of the temple: both rabbinic Judaism and the church, each in its own way, superseded that Israel—to use the dangerous expression.

The Judaism of the time between return from exile and the destruction of AD 70 was a congeries of what we can only call "denominations," united mostly by the sacrificial cult of the Jerusalem temple. Those groups survived the Temple's destruction that could if necessary do without it. The Pharisaic movement developed into rabbinic Judaism, centered on the study of Torah and the practice of the specific laws by which Jewish identity is maintained; if necessary, both could be pursued anywhere. And the Jesus movement had a ubiquitous temple in the eucharistic body of the risen Christ (John 2:20–21). Thus rabbinic Judaism's and the church's ways of obeying old Israel's Scripture are parallel and analogously problematic.

Eventually, each in the new situation fully submitted to the Scripture by adding a second volume: the rabbis added the Mishnah and the church the New Testament. It is these second volumes that thereafter, and with equal historical and theological legitimacy, determine each community's way of reading Tanakh/Old Testament. The Mishnah is a legal complex; and rabbinic Judaism reads the Tanakh fundamentally as Torah, given theological-historical context by the nonlegal writings. The New Testament tells and comments a story that claims to culminate one told by the Old Testament; and the church reads the Old Testament fundamentally as narrative history with this telos, given its moral structure by Torah.

The decisive second-century history was certainly more complicated than the previous statements of principle might suggest. Historically speaking, that the church would persevere in reading the Old Testament canon as narrative, or indeed in obeying it as in any way a functioning canon, was by no means assured. And it was always the law that was the problem (Campenhausen, *Entstehung*, 30–46).

24 Paul's defense of Gentile believers' freedom from the law had been done by narrative reading of the Old Testament: the promise to Abraham, and his righteousness by faith in the promise, came

first, and the law was given later, so that the law had its function within a relation to God fundamentally determined not by it but by the earlier and foundational giving of the promise (Gal. 3:16–19). Thus Paul distinguished historically related and theologically differentiated periods in God's relation to his people, and could proclaim the inclusion of the Gentiles-as-Gentiles as a new event within the one history.

But in the soon overwhelmingly Gentile church, freedom from Old Testament ritual and purity laws quickly came to be so taken for granted that the problem was no longer felt. When the law again became a problem, the worry ran the other way around: If the Old Testament is full of laws that do not apply, many of which indeed seem merely bizarre, how can this book be Scripture? What can be the matter with eating shrimp? If the Old Testament mandates circumcision for all would-be inheritors of Abraham, and our apostle forbade Gentile believers to be circumcised, how is the Old Testament authoritative Scripture?

In the mid-second century, three events more or less coincided: "the gnostic crisis," earlier noted; Marcion's passionate insistence that the Old Testament's God could not possibly be the Father of Jesus; and the intellectual dominance of Gentile converts with a little—always indeed a dangerous thing—Middle-Platonist education. Together, these raised the issue with force.

Gnostic theologians saw clearly how the Old Testament's story of Israel and Israel's law was firmly set in this world; their passion to escape this world and its ills necessarily mandated drastic reimagining of both Israel and its law. Quite differently, Marcion's rejection of the Old Testament resulted from taking it absolutely seriously in what a modern exegete might call its "own" and "original" sense: the law, he said, is the law of the Jews, who indeed have to obey it, but not of the Christians, since they do not. The God who gave this harsh law, and had created the imperfect world in which it was necessary, is the God of this world and of the Jews and clearly has quite another character than the Father of Jesus. Or we may put it so: as this monomaniacal Paulinist read the letters of "*the* apostle," the law and the gospel of Christ became for him simple contraries. Finally, Middle Platonism's spiritualizing and elitist enlightenment, shared by some Christian theologians, was bound to boggle at the earthy realism of the law and of the Old Testament's stories of the people of the law.

25

So far as we know, it was Justin the Martyr, writing around 150, who renewed a history-of-salvation construal of the Old Testament—now not to defend the freedom of the gospel in view of the Old Testament, but rather to defend the Old Testament in view of the gospel. According to Justin, the Old Testament's various sorts of now-inapplicable law are not therefore to be denied divine and salvific authority. They had not always been inapplicable, but had their salvific roles in a previous period of the one God's one history with his creation (*Dialogue with Trypho* 10–29). Thus the commandment of circumcision was necessary in its time, to mark the separation and unique dedication of Israel. But within the total plot of God's continuing history with his people, that time is not the time of the church, of the Israel that welcomes Gentiles as Gentiles.

This general approach became and remained the standard argument of the mostly Gentile church. But while this approach is doubtless correct so far as it goes, it does not quite eliminate the problem. It is open to the error that we began by rejecting: it can be and has been taken to imply that the covenant of the Old Testament is simply surpassed by the gospel. Justin himself was an ardent supersessionist.

CHAPTER 3

Creed and the
Old Testament

As Irenaeus perceived, the gnostics, however dangerously attractive they might be in a religious culture that loved elaborate myths and supposedly elite secrets, were in principle rather easily dispatched, at least among the judicious: you had only to describe their opinions, which Irenaeus does in wearisome detail. Particularly, the way gnostic apologists used Scripture was too obviously arbitrary to survive much exposure. Irenaeus likened the gnostics' biblical exegesis to taking a mosaic apart and then using the tesserae to construct an entirely different picture, drawn from a vision alien to that for which the tesserae were cut (*Against Heresies* 1.8.1). The gnostics' credibility problem was that anyone who knew the Scripture and the *regula fidei* could survey both pictures and see the trick being done. And in any case, the gnostics regarded their teaching as indeed on a higher revelatory niveau than that of the church, but not as necessarily contrary to it; accordingly, they usually did not regard the Old Testament as simply false but merely as inferior and in need of illumination by a higher wisdom.

Marcion was the life-and-death opponent: "Only this man was openly so bold as to mutilate the Scriptures and to defame God" (Irenaeus, *Against Heresies* 1.27.4). If the church and its Scripture were to be saved for each other, Marcion was the one to refute.

For one thing, Marcion was forthright: he did not play games with the Old Testament canon; he simply rejected it. For another,

27

his rejection was based on principle: the Jews are right in reading their Scripture as law—who after all should better know how to read it? But the gospel is a message of freedom from law. Finally, Marcion not only rejected the church's existing Scripture; he also proposed the Scripture that a true church would have had, composed of Pauline and Lukan—in his view, secondarily Pauline—writings, edited, to be sure, to remove allegedly spurious passages that approved the Old Testament or its law and had stolen in even there.

Did Marcion in the process make and promote the first explicit Christian canon? Whether or not Marcion called it that? This was the older view (Campenhausen, *Entstehung*, 175); more recently it has been questioned (Allert, *High View?* 89–93); the difference is perhaps terminological. Marcion certainly did explicitly reject the existing Old Testament canon and propose a definite set of other documents in its place.

It was not impossible that the gentile church should have followed Marcion; indeed there were for generations Marcionite congregations that thought of themselves as the church reformed according to Jesus' and Paul's original gospel and that proselytized for this reformation. It was the rule of faith that saved the church from abandoning its founding canon.

Marcion identified the Old Testament with the flawed creation that needed law; and whatever problems the mostly Gentile church otherwise had with the Old Testament, it could not let go the doctrine of creation. For this was intrinsic to its founding communal consciousness: as far back as we can identify statements of the rule of faith, they insist on the Creator and the goodness of his work. Indeed, when opposing Marcion and the gnostics, Irenaeus can produce statements of the rule that speak *only* of creation. Thus, "the rule [*regula*] of the truth that we hold is this: There is one God Almighty, who created all things through his word. He both prepared and made all things out of nothing." Then follows mention of the Son and Spirit as and only as the Creator's mediators in that work (Irenaeus, *Against Heresies* 1.22.1). This version may have been tailored to the case, or it may have been ready at hand.

So far so good. But now we must consider a problem, signaled by the following observation. A less-blinkered Marcion might have noticed that in the Old Testament itself the theological center of gravity, with respect to the role of the law, is not creation as such but

28

the exodus and the revelation at Sinai. What if Marcion had leveled his chief attack not against the creation, on account of its imperfections and consequent need for the law, but against the Old Testament stories of the very giving of the law? It might have been an effective polemic, for the tales of exodus and Sinai were guaranteed to offend the more sophisticated versions of antiquity's religious sensibility: consider only the story of the Israelite elders' cheerful dinner party with God on the mountain (Exod. 24:11), or of Moses' view of God's "back parts". (33:23 in the more unabashed KJV). Would the rule of faith have so strongly summoned the church to meet an attack centered here?

The rule of faith insists that the Father of Jesus is indeed the Creator, but that is its only usual Old Testament reference; one of Tertullian's versions is a laudable exception (text in Schaff, *Creeds*, 2:19). Thus the rule did not support the church's native way of reading the Old Testament, as history. In defending the law, Justin had taught churchly theology to perceive differing periods within God's relationship with his people, thereby reactivating the church's primordially demanded historical reading of the Old Testament. But this teaching did not enter the rule of faith, which skipped straight from the creation to the incarnation, and thus right over the whole of God's history with old Israel; if anything, the confrontation with Marcion may have solidified this habit. And the developed baptismal creeds have followed the pattern: "I believe in God the Father Almighty, Creator of heaven and earth. And in Jesus Christ his only Son, our Lord, who was conceived. . . ."

The rule of faith saved the Old Testament as canon for the church—or rather, the church for the Old Testament canon—but in the process it did not open itself to the theological shape of the Old Testament's own narrative, and so it could not support the Old Testament's specific role in the church's practice. And support was and is needed: the leap from creation to New Testament appeared and continues to appear at other key places in the church's life. Thus, for example, for centuries Western orders for the regular Eucharist specified no reading from the Old Testament. And until the most recent liturgical reforms, nearly all Western eucharistic prayers made the same leap as the creeds do, from creation and perhaps the fall to the New Testament story.

How are we to account for the creedal tradition's leap from creation to Mary's conception of Jesus? Also as it is propagated in liturgy and theology? As with all historical phenomena, there are no doubt many causes. We cannot exclude the prejudices of the Gentile believers who carried the strand of the tradition that survived and comes to us. The doctrine of creation is about all humanity, without particular reference to Israel—or so it can be made to appear—whereas the exodus and the revelation at Sinai are, also in the church's christological reading of the texts, events in the history of a particular people, with whom the mostly Gentile church had an at-best uneasy relation.

Missionary practice may have played a role. The rule of faith was, among other functions, a memorandum of points that the gospel message had to touch, and as apologetics in the Gentile mission, creation must often have seemed the place to begin, while the exodus and Sinai were unpromising. Thus in the Athenian sermon attributed to Paul in Acts, the point of attachment with his hearers is the existence of the world, and his message begins with proclamation of the God responsible for it (Acts 17:24–27). In places like Athens, creation could be presented as novel but nevertheless more or less comprehensible religious wisdom, whereas the exodus or the history of Israel's travails could only with strenuous reimagining be presented in that light.

Finally, the shock jointly delivered by Marcion and the gnostics will surely have concentrated churchly minds at the point of their main attack, to the exclusion of other concerns. It certainly focused Irenaeus's mind: chapter upon repetitive chapter of his defense of church teaching is devoted to proving, by whatever exegetical means come to hand, that the Creator and the Father of Jesus are "the same God," who "in all things and through all things . . . is shown forth: who created man, and promised the inheritance of the earth to the patriarchs, who extended the promise to the resurrection of the just, and realized the promises in the reign of the Son" (*Against Heresies* 5.36.3). Note that here the promises to the Old Testament patriarchs are instanced, which do not appear when the rule of faith itself is stated.

If the church's primordial way of reading the Old Testament is right, then Christ's work both concludes and includes the revelation in old Israel. The time of creed making is in most churches' and theologians' judgment finished, but as a hypothesis contrary to fact, one can think of a creed whose second article would have begun, "and in Jesus Christ, his only Son, our Lord, who as the Word given to Moses led Israel out of Egypt . . ."

The lack of Old Testament narrative in the creedal tradition occasioned a lamentable development in nineteenth- and twentieth-century theology, whose ill effects continue to be felt. The lacuna was an open door for a recrudescence of Marcion's question: Can the God of the Old Testament really be the God of Jesus Christ? Most "Neoprotestant" theology accepted with the creed that Jesus' Father is indeed the Creator, the God of Genesis 1–2, though what some strands of Neoprotestantism meant by "creation" is another matter. But is not the God who appears in the Old Testament's further narrative a warlike, judgmental, and even cruel God? Who is utterly unlike the loving Father of Jesus?

When the narratives of the patriarchs' adventures, of the exodus, of the conquest of Canaan, or of the Lord's judgments and restorations of Israel are felt as alien, one of two things is likely to happen; both have actually happened, and both undermine the faith.

One possible and currently actual outcome is that preaching and teaching construe "the New Testament's God" simply by constructing a contrary of the supposed Old Testament God: the God of the gospel is pacific, nonjudgmental, and in general a really nice person. In much of the liberal church, in many Evangelical groups, and indeed among many "progressive" Catholics, theology has thus been replaced by sentimentality: God is not so much fatherly as grandfatherly, endlessly "accepting" and "inclusive."

The other outcome is that the function of the Old Testament's depiction of God is taken over by an alternative depiction ready and waiting in the tradition: the divine reality posited by the Western Enlightenment in the ever-continuing train of Aristotle and the other great pagan Greek theologians. Aristotle's "most excellent" "divine existence" is perfect just in that there is no potentiality in it, nothing it could be that it has not eternally been. To be thus pure of potentiality, this God must be pure of all relation to temporal beings; they can be related to it, but it cannot be related to them. In Aristotle, the perfect divine existence is a presupposition of the world's existence and perdurance, but it has never done and never does anything to be that presupposition. This God is a state of pure self-absorption.

If the New Testament's references to God are thought to refer to such a static Perfection, then everything that the New Testament

31

says *about* God—that he sends the Christ, that he gives over Christ to the powers of the world, that he raises Christ from the death to which these powers condemn him, and so forth—in its obvious unsuitability to a divine Inactivity, must be endlessly explained. And because the explanation is indeed endless because hopeless, finally all will be explained away. Preachers and teachers of all confessional groupings have for centuries labored mightily at this lamentable task.

We have arrived again at a point to which, as also in the following, we will repeatedly come: the canon without the creed will not serve to protect the church against perversion of the gospel, *and* neither will the creed without the canon. Perhaps even the two together will not finally serve without the third leg, a sacramentally constituted continuity of church governance. There will be a quick chapter about that.

CHAPTER 4

New Testament Canon and *Regula Fidei*

The time from the death of the apostles to shortly before Irenaeus's writing was characterized by "the lack of a formal guarantee of the tradition that . . . testifies to Christ; the lack, that is . . . , of a New Testament." This "condition of unreflected trust" in the church's immediate possession of the faith "could not last forever, and one may find it odd that it lasted as long as it did" (Campenhausen, *Entstehung*, 173–74).

Irenaeus, writing in the later second century, could still understand himself as the inhabitant of a community that embraced him in the original apostolic witness; and in speaking to the faithful in the ordinary way of preaching and teaching, he continued to need no other Scripture than the Old Testament. But to combat the polemics of Marcion and the seduction of the gnostics, this practice no longer sufficed. For Marcion too supposed that the church's tradition reached back to Jesus' immediate followers, and charged that it was this very tradition, starting with the Twelve themselves, that had falsified Jesus' gospel—perhaps in his youth Marcion had been impressed by an abrupt round of the telephone game. As for the gnostics, they were only too eager to bandy community traditions.

Against such attacks on the church's tradition, Irenaeus summoned what we can only call biblical proof texts to establish the identity of the church's teaching with the original message.

33

Decisively for our interest, he drew them from the Old Testament *and* from the writings that make our New Testament. These writings were his arsenal, and we can watch them consolidate as he uses them. A truly dedicated scholar has counted the Scripture proofs in *Against Heresies*: he tells us that there are 1,694 of them; the great majority are from writings that would shortly be called the New Testament (Campenhausen, *Entstehung,* 217).

Moreover, against the heretics Irenaeus uses the Gospels and apostolic letters precisely and consciously as touchstone *documents* of the original message. Thus the famous manifesto of the basis on which he will stand against false teachers: "The Lord of all gave his apostles authority to proclaim the gospel. . . . Nor have we learned the economy of our salvation from any others. . . . Moreover, in accord with God's will, they later transmitted it to us in writings, to be the future foundation and pillar of our faith" (*Against Heresies* 3.Preface.1.1). Irenaeus thus straightforwardly treats the available collections of Gospels and apostolic letters as a specific sort of Scripture, and in the course of his arguments he will defend even such things as his Gospel collection's quaternity as divinely necessary (3.11.8–9).

One may wonder what the probative value of these documents can be since it is precisely the reliability of most of their authors that Marcion and the gnostics had put in question. Irenaeus's argument, as sketched above, is indeed circular: we may be sure of the apostolic writings' truth because they come from those from whom "we learned the economy of our salvation." That is, we are to trust the presence of truth in the community because it is confirmed by the Gospels and apostolic letters; and we are to trust these documents because they come from those whose witness forms the community. Canon confirms creed, and creed confirms canon. The circle is not, however, vicious, for the argument is aimed not to convince the heretics themselves but to reassure those living in that very community; the argument is warranted by the community's life and the intended readers' envelopment in it. Confidence in apostolic documents as a guarantor of the gospel emerges from the earliest church's immediate awareness of her truth, at the last moment when that awareness could by itself settle the issue.

34   The earliest of the documents that would become the New Testament are the Letters of Paul. Given the underlying need— the telephone-game problem—they were inevitable chief candi-

dates to be the new kind of Scripture when it should be needed. They labored under a certain theological disadvantage that we will shortly note, but otherwise they were just what would be wanted: a substantial body of explicitly pastoral and theological writings, which were reliably known to be from one of the apostles. If Paul's literary legacy could not be a documentary touchstone of gospel authenticity, what could?

Our contemporary short way with letters was not the practice of antiquity. Thus, while Paul indeed wrote his letters to deal with particular situations, it will nevertheless have been understood that they would be read and reread, that copies would be made, and that these could be exchanged between recipients. Reading Paul or hearing him read, one often wonders how his initial readers and hearers can possibly have followed some of his reasonings; but Paul did not have to reckon with a single exposure; he could count on his letters being studied and argued about and restudied and so on.

Did Paul then intend his letters as in some sense Scripture for his congregations? This is not intrinsically implausible, given Paul's understanding of himself as an immediate messenger of Christ. Paul could not, however, have thought of his letters as Scripture in the here relevant senses, nor could any other apostle. His letters were after all not antecedent to his own Christian existence, and for all his consciousness of uniqueness, he was a fellow member in the church; therefore he could not regard his letters as antecedently foundational for the church, in the fashion of the Old Testament. Nor had so much time gone by that he could think of the church as temporally extended in the way that would later require documentary touchstones of the gospel's diachronic identity.

Yet he wrote because he thought—quite bluntly in the case of the Galatians—that even in the church's passing moment, falling away from the true gospel was a possibility, and one that he could combat by writing. This again suggests his possible intent to supply authoritative scripture; but again we must rest with a negative judgment. As Paul himself makes plain, his need to write arose from a missionary pastor's inability to be at more than one place at a time, so that the letters are *substitutes* for the personal address that would have been the proper mode for what he had to say (e.g., 2 Cor. 10:11). Putting forward such emergency measures as Scripture, however carefully and self-consciously wrought they were in themselves, surely lay outside the possible scope of his intention.

35

But did perhaps the congregations who first received and preserved and exchanged Paul's writings nevertheless treat them as Scripture? That is, did they use them as they used the old Scripture, citing them to justify the gospel? So far as the evidence lets us see, this did not happen until some decades later. On the contrary, the earliest preserved external reference to Paul's letters (2 Pet. 3:16), from a time when his letters could be thought of as among "the writings"—whatever time that was and whatever that phrase may then have denoted—warns against their use in such a capacity, as ecclesially and doctrinally as much a part of the problem as a help with it—again, whatever the current problem was.

Thus the circulating letters of Paul were not at first Scripture, but instead were ready and waiting to be made Scripture, so soon as there was a felt need for the kind of documentary assurance they could provide. Or rather, so soon as that need was so strongly felt as to overcome suspicion of Paul's sometimes gnostic-sounding theologoumena. For one could reasonably ask, to take only one instance, "What is this 'wisdom'—*sophia*, the very name of the key divine emanation in some gnostic systems!—that Paul shares only with 'the mature,' and that is 'not of this *aiōn*'—other words popular with gnostics? (1 Cor. 2:6)." For Paul's letters to be Scripture, they would have to be set in a wider apostolic context, to balance their liability to unfortunate interpretation—and we may even think that this continues to be the case.

The other chief group of writings waiting to be Scripture was the Gospels. Almost everything about their initial history is disputed and probably destined to remain that way. That Mark, if we may so name the author, produced the first such writing is the well-founded standard opinion of modern scholarship. But the formerly usual opinion that Mark created a new literary genre is now strongly disputed: Mark's Gospel and the others can be shown to display many formal marks of Hellenistic antiquity's *bios*, the celebratory life of a great man (in accessible summary: Bauckham, *Testimony*, 93–112).

If Mark was indeed first, it is clear that Matthew and Luke used him and added material from other sources. Among those other sources, was there another and prior "Gospel" of a different sort, which scholars have labeled "Q," a collection of Jesus' sayings that presented these as in themselves salvific? The matter is disputed and will probably continue to be. And how are we to sort out John's

36

relation to the other Gospels, or its own redactional history? Finally, who wrote any of these works? The names traditionally given as authors are not claimed in the works themselves.

It would be helpful if we had reliable answers to these questions; since we do not, we must do without. Rough dating is, however, needed and possible. Mark can surely be dated shortly before the fall of Jerusalem in 70 and is usually placed around 65—though again, a few dissent. The other Gospels must then follow between the fall of Jerusalem and the end of the century.

As to the specific purpose for which each of the Gospels was written, this is yet another standing occasion for scholarly ingenuity. But something else about them *is* clear: their *logical* relation to the gospel message itself; and it is this relation that, it seems to me, is decisive for their eventual canonical role.

The shortest possible statement of the gospel is "Jesus is risen." The proposition displays a straightforward logic. "Jesus" identifies who is risen, and this identification is essential to the character of the message: "Hitler is risen" would be good news to few. Then the predicate "is risen" attributes to this Jesus the salvific significance that Israel's prophetic tradition and much Second-Temple Judaism had packed into the hope of resurrection.

Identification by proper names alone often fails: we may say, "John is sick," and be met with "And who is that?" Our normal response will be what we may call identifying narrative: "John is the one who sold me my house, who ushers at our church, and who . . ." until the identification penny drops.

For a time the name "Jesus" was notorious in Galilee and Judea, but narrative identification was soon needed. We may imagine a dialogue: "Jesus is risen!" "And so? Who is that?" "He is a prophet, who preached the immediacy of the kingdom, who healed the sick, who befriended publicans and sinners, who . . ." and so on until Jesus' perceived identity is thick enough for ". . . is risen" to be morally and spiritually specific news.

Mark's creation has exactly this logical form. Whatever ancient literary genres may have shaped his rhetorical moves and structures, and whatever sources may have provided his material, his Gospel as written is *logically* a single long proposition of the form "Jesus, the one who . . . and who . . . and who . . . is risen." Whatever Mark's immediate purpose in writing may have been, the text he produced served that purpose by expanding the proposition "Jesus is risen" for narrative identification of the subject and for dramatic insistence on the predicate. The same can be said, mutatis mutandis, of the other now-canonical Gospels.

Each Gospel's selection, editing, and arrangement of identifying items of the narrative reflect the theological bents of its antecedent tradents and of its author and possible editor, and the exigencies of their various ecclesial context or contexts. Discerning these is a theologically central task of exegetical scholarship, since the theologies of such primal witnesses must have great weight in the church's continuing theological discussion and debate. But it is the logical form that here concerns us: the Gospels offer themselves to be Scripture precisely because, as extended narrative identifications of the risen one and as peremptory proclamations of his resurrection, they are not tied to the immediate catechetical or polemical or missionary needs in service of which their authors may have composed them.

So long as the church perdures past those days of "unreflected trust," the question will always be urgent, "Who is risen?" For the apostolic answer, we will have to turn to the Gospels. And the church will regularly need to be reminded that the founding salvific predicate is ". . . is risen," and not some other; again, the Gospels are the best reminders.

For decades, Gospels circulated among the congregations both separately and in combinations. Even in response to Marcion, there seems to have been no concerted attempt directly to counter what he did, by in turn settling on a single Gospel—which would undoubtedly have been Matthew—and so on a standard narrative and its theological bent. Thus a plurality of Gospels remained, despite the embarrassment posed by disagreements between them (Campenhausen, *Entstehung*, 200–201). Some attempts were indeed made to combine available Gospels into a single harmony Gospel; one such, Tatian's *Diatessaron*, even became the canonical Gospel of an otherwise orthodox wing of the church, but the future did not lie with such devices.

By the time Irenaeus set himself to arm believers against temptation by the gnostics and Marcion, the collection of Matthew, Mark, Luke, and John had sorted itself out and was at hand, at least in his precincts of the church. This collection provided Irenaeus with his primary guarantee of the authentic words and deeds of the Lord himself, and with other apostolic testimony to provide context

38

for that of Paul. As for the problem of narrative variation among the four, his resolution is strictly theological—indeed a priori—and is nicely caught by his phrase for the collection, "the fourfold Gospel," with its plurally referring adjective and singularly referring noun (*Against Heresies* 3.5.1). There is by definition one gospel, which by the providence of God has taken the form of four Gospels. This could happen because the apostles "all together and each of them singly possessed the gospel of God" (3.1.1). And if we are not always able to make their accounts fully agree, Irenaeus will simply not worry about it.

Next we must take note of Acts. As the second volume of Luke's work, it almost automatically came along with the four Gospels. In Irenaeus's refutation of the heretics, it had two roles (Campenhausen, *Entstehung*, 234–36). It provided some access to the witness of apostles other than Paul. And just so it tied the two great parts of Irenaeus's New Testament together, displaying Paul among and in ultimate harmony with other apostles—a purpose, by the way, that modern critical study sometimes detects in the work itself.

Thus Irenaeus indeed worked with what can only be called a New Testament canon. And his canon and its theological rationale were inherited and developed by such late second- and early third-century theologians as Tertullian and Origen, for both of whom a Christian Scripture in two parts was already a given. In Clement of Alexandria, active at the turn of the century and himself not much of a biblical scholar, we find the first documentation of the names "Old Testament" and "New Testament" (Campenhausen, *Entstehung*, 339). When did the church have a functioning canon of Old and New Testaments? At or shortly before the turn of the third century.

This century was then occupied in tidying up, mostly by drawing necessary limits. Precisely because it was now established that Christian writings could be Scripture, one had to decide which of the inherited writings—of which there was by now a small library—could claim that status.

It was reliable witness to the original message that was required for inclusion in the new second volume of Scripture. Thus we may, as has usually been done, say that "apostolicity" was the criterion. But this notion must not be taken in a too-wooden fashion; to see this, we need only observe that Mark and Luke were known not to have been apostles. How then could Irenaeus and the others

39

include their putative writings in the fourfold Gospel? To be sure, they supposed—or decreed—that Mark was Peter's pupil and Luke was Paul's. But the basic warrant lay elsewhere, in the *regula fidei*. Assurance that these writings did in historical fact derive from apostolic days was indeed a necessary condition, but what finally sustained Mark and Luke—and other writings of doubtful provenance—was recognition that they witnessed to the apostolic faith as it lived in the church. Thus again we must note that the relation between the Gospel canon and the creedal tradition was, as it still is, circular; the church recognizes authentic Gospels by coherence with its living grasp of the apostolic faith; and against deviation from that faith, it summons those Gospels as apostolic witness. In this circularity a more dogmatic essay might see occasion to discuss the Holy Spirit, as Irenaeus actually does (*Against Heresies* 3.24.1).

The acknowledged main blocks of a New Testament were thus the four Gospels and Paul's Letters. The decisions to be made were about writings that trailed after these, as in our New Testament some still do. Such documents as the *Apocalypse of Peter* or the Shepherd of Hermas, which some churches had read in their worship, were by common consent demoted to the status of edifying literature. Others that had been suspect, such as the book of Hebrews, about whose authorship there had been a parade of acknowledged guesses, finally asserted their place. The Johannine literature underwent critique on suspicion of gnosticism, but survived. For our purposes we do not need to follow this history in further detail.

Two inseparable questions need further consideration: What provoked the consolidation of a New Testament Scripture? And what steered the process toward the particular New Testament we in fact have? Neither the fact nor the shape of the new Scripture was Irenaeus's single-handed theological achievement, as our presentation so far may suggest. Even Campenhausen, who perhaps credits too much to Irenaeus, calls him "only the path-breaking representative of a work of disposition and reflection that responded to a generally felt urgent need" (Campenhausen, *Entstehung*, 245).

The midcentury coincidence of crises was undoubtedly the provoking cause of that urgent feeling. But would a New Testament Scripture have shortly emerged if there had been no Marcionite critique and no gnostic seducers? Probably, for the telephone-game problem is intrinsic to historically continuous communities, and in the case of the church, action to deal with it was in any case overdue. Without being steered by the particular antignostic theology of Irenaeus and his immediate successors, would it have been this same canon? A different history might have shaped a different canon, but since history contrary to fact is imponderable, so is that canon.

We return to what actually happened. We cannot claim that the *regula fidei* actively shaped the very New Testament that came about. On the contrary, the material relation between the creedal tradition and the new canon is at first glance problematic. The creedal tradition provides little or no narrative of Christ's teachings and deeds; it thus suggests, if anything, that the church could get along without it—which is to say, without Gospels. The creedal tradition, taken in itself, brings little theological reflection to the first article's concept of creation, or to the events the second article narrates, or to the sanctifying contexts of which the third article tells us; thus it suggests, if anything, that the church could get along without such reflections as occupy Paul's Letters; the theological interpolations into the creed appropriated at Nicaea serve purposes other than those that creed served in its native baptismal role.

But we should take a second look, from the other side. As we have said, around the middle of the second century, the church found something intolerably lacking. We have so far stipulated that "something" rather generally. Now let me suggest that what was more specifically lacking was support for those essential aspects of the message that the *regula fidei* did not—as our creeds still do not—directly support. One cannot, for example, forever keep saying, "Jesus died to save us from our sin," without pondering how that might work, without the kind of second-level reflection that Paul exemplifies. Thus sophisticated theological reflection à la Paul or the evangelist John belongs to the mission itself. One cannot keep confessing, for example, "He is Lord," without helpfully identifying the subject. Thus to remain gospel, the gospel narrative requires narrative expansion, à la the Gospels.

Looked at from this angle, the new canon and the rule of faith match like conversely notched puzzle pieces. Each advances what the other holds back. Canon and creed fitted together, and only canon and creed fitted together, could make and can now make one whole and integral guardian of the church's temporal self-identity.

41

CHAPTER 5

The Apostles' Creed

In the Western church, the paradigm of a full-fledged creed is "the Apostles' Creed," and this creed will be the matter of the present chapter—though in following chapters we will sometimes adduce also the dominant creed of the East, the Niceno-Constantinopolitan Creed. The Apostles' Creed's attribution to an apostolic conclave, where each of the Twelve is supposed to have contributed one clause, is obviously legendary; but the development of the legend and the popular title followed a true intuition. For this text is indeed a sort of final version of the *regula fidei* (see comparative tables in Schaff, *Creeds*, 2:40–41, 52–55), structured on the pattern of the early baptismal questions.

The Apostles' Creed now in use is a rather late version of the baptismal-catechetical creed of Rome, which became the creed of the West as the church of Rome spread its discipline to all churches on the territory of the former Western empire (for the history, see Kelly, *Creeds*, 398–434). It is generally supposed that the earliest surely identifiable version of the text is one that can be reconstructed from citations in a work of 404 by Rufinus of Aquileia; an almost identical creed, not explicitly identified as Roman but plausibly to be located there, appears in a work from sixty years earlier (texts in Kelly, *Creeds*, 102–3). The text's prehistory in versions of the *regula fidei* and of the baptismal questions can be followed back to the end of the second century.

43

The text of this "Old Roman" creed, as it is usually called (on the following, see Kelly, *Creeds*, 372–74), lacks praise of the Father as Creator; this was evidently the case also in much of its earlier history. Why it is omitted is not apparent since in East and West alike the *regula fidei* insisted on creation. With this omission the last vestige of explicit Old Testament reference disappears. Less surprisingly, this text also lacks Christ's descent to "the regions of the dead" (*ad inferna*), description of the church as "catholic," and communion with "the saints."

The descent to the place of the dead begins to appear in fifth-century variations of the Roman creed, having been a popular theological topic in the East for centuries. Its appearance in creeds may initially have simply been a final emphasis on the reality of the Lord's death: after crucifixion and burial, he was in the same place as the rest of the dead. But from quite early, beginning indeed with 1 Peter 3:19, there had been theological discussion of what he did there during the three days before his resurrection to new life (for patristic proposals, see Kelly, *Creeds*, 378–83). Was he, as in 1 Peter, proclaiming the good news to the saints among the dead? Or was he actually accomplishing the defeat of death, as he had earned it by his endurance of the cross, breaking down the gates of death's realm, as in much wonderful Eastern iconography? Or as in some Reformation and contemporary Catholic thought, was he enduring the final and deepest pain of his own death? One will, I fear, have to construe the three days according to the construal of the salvific relation between the Lord's crucifixion and resurrection found in one's theological tradition and own best reflection. I confess my own leaning toward the theology of the Eastern icons, which is not that of my own tradition.

That the church is "catholic," as a coherent and embracing whole, poses no such problems—and "catholic" is not in the creed a pole to "Protestant." Given the doctrine's primal and general currency and its secure place in Eastern creeds, its inclusion in the Western creed was only a matter of time. About the "communion of saints," *communio sanctorum*, there is a notorious problem: since *sanctorum* can be either masculine or neuter, the phrase can mean either "fellowship with the [departed] saints" or "fellowship in holy things [i.e., the sacraments]." It seems clear to me that at this place in the creed, the phrase intends the former (for the arguments, see Kelly, *Creeds*, 388–97). And we may, while we are at it, note that

44

both the Old Roman creed and the Latin texts of the current text have the resurrection "of the flesh" (*carnis*) and not "of the body," the latter being introduced only by squeamish English translators; contrast the German translation, *Auferstehung des Fleisches*. For the rest, the Old Roman creed is the Apostles' Creed now in use.

In a previous chapter we anticipated the first and most obvious thing to be said about the Apostles' Creed: it is shaped to the name of the God into whose obedience new Christians are initiated (Matt. 28:19). For Christ's mandate to baptize indeed specifies a single personal proper name, apt to identify a particular God. The triadic "Father . . . Son . . . Spirit" is not a *collection* of names. Rather, the three names make the internal structure of one name, which names the church's God from the plot of his history with us, a plot represented by biblical names for the dramatis personae of the story. God is God the Father as the author and ruler of his history with us; God's personal presence as an actor in the story he writes is, in train particularly of John's language, God the Son; and God the Spirit is the Spirit who from Genesis 1:2 onward appears in Scripture as God's own liveliness, liberating creatures to be other actors in God's history. "Father," "Son," and "Spirit" here make an internal structure of the one God's personal name, which displays the great biblical claim that God's history with his people is not only their history but also his own, that he truly is in his one self the Father, Son, and Spirit of saving history. Precisely by and in their distinctions from one another, the three identities are one God; thus their names, by evoking these distinctions, are one name.

By virtue of the name's import, just sketched, and by virtue of the name's canonically mandated place in baptism, "Father, Son, and Holy Spirit" must even be accounted *the* Christian name for God, in continuation of YHWH in the Old Testament. Nevertheless, schismatic movements have sometimes, for one reason or another, replaced the name with other formulas. Thus in the latter decades of the past century, some feminists supposed that calling God "Father" resulted from projecting into eternity a human role that men assert, while not similarly elevating feminine roles; this led to substitution of allegedly gender-free formulas like "Creator, Redeemer, and Sanctifier." Some were actually baptized with such formulas.

Such proposals depend on not observing, or perhaps suppressing, two rather obvious points. First, the triadic name is indeed a

45

proper name, that intends to identify which of the many candidates to be God is invoked at baptism; whereas "Creator, Redeemer, and Sanctifier" and all similar formulas are collections of theological predicates that can identify no one, since most alleged gods will claim these characteristics. Nor are such collections inherently trinitarian since there is no reason to stop with three predicates; more could be added and indeed indefinitely. Second and most decisive, the import of the three inner names does *not* reside in any descriptive meaning of each one separately, but solely in the internal logic by which they make one name.

Within the one name's internal logic, designation of God's first identity as "Father" is not a projection of values thought to be generally resident in fatherhood; rather, God is Father as and only as he is related to a specific someone, Jesus the Christ, in a way for which filiation is the created analogue. As to why it is "Father" rather than "Mother," it is because Jesus as a faithful Jew spoke to and about God in that way, and because it is only in unison with him that we are at all permitted to address or invoke God in filial fashion. No doubt this is historically a contingency, but it is a contingency of the same order as God's choice of the Jews instead of my ancestral Scandinavians, or the Son's incarnation as Jesus of Nazareth instead of as, say, Bar Kokhba.

Again, designation of the second identity as "Son" does not affix a general label for divine emanations; rather, God is Son as he relates to the one who by virtue of that same relation is called his Father. The circle is precisely the point. And yet again, designation of the third identity as "Spirit" does not come from that foggy realm of human religiosity that is now likely to be called "spirituality"; instead, God is Spirit as he is the spirit of the Father's and the Son's mutuality, as he is Love and gives himself to be the love between the Father and the Son, so that they can be pure love for one another and so actually be one God.

Next we must observe that Matthew's mandate of the name "Father, Son, and Holy Spirit" for baptism is only one, though pivotal, instance of what I have elsewhere dubbed the New Testament's "primary trinitarianism" (Jenson, *Theology*, 1:91–94). It is often supposed that the doctrine of Trinity was imposed upon the plain sense of Scripture; this opinion can be maintained only by ignoring the way Scripture's God-language actually works, and the actual course of trinitarian reflection. In later chapters we will briefly look

46

at the Old Testament's quite overt trinitarianism (at greater length, Jenson, *Theology*, 1:75–89), and at the trinitarian creed's necessary guidance in reading the New Testament; here we record a logic that constrains the New Testament's habits of language.

When the writers of the New Testament, within all strands of its authorship, mention God in specific connection with their gospel, they are with rare exceptions driven to touch, in one way or another, the three dramatic bases pointed to by the triune name's mutual inner references. Here I give only a tiny sampling, drawn at some random from various New Testament traditions. "Be filled with the Spirit, . . . giving thanks to God the Father . . . in the name of our Lord Jesus Christ" (Eph. 5:18–20). "Pray in the Holy Spirit; keep yourselves in the love of God; look forward to the mercy of our Lord Jesus Christ" (Jude 20–21). "Grace to you and peace from him who is and who was and who is to come, and from the seven spirits who are before his throne, and from Jesus Christ" (Rev. 1:4–5). And we must mention Paul's famous benediction: "The grace of the Lord Jesus Christ, and the love of God, and the fellowship of the Holy Spirit be with you all" (2 Cor. 13:14 RSV).

Here one bit of scholarly polemics must intrude, for the sake of any who may follow this book's references and read further. Cullmann's discussion of the earliest confessional formulas (*Confessions*, 35ff.) is unreliable, due to naiveté about how various sorts of language function in the actual life of the church. An amusing but indicative gaffe appears in a footnote saying that the "trinitarian declarations in the New Testament," since they have "a liturgical character," cannot count as "confessions of faith" (36).

In developed trinitarian reflection, God is said to be one God as and only as he is the three identities that are that God, each established in and only in its relation to the other two. Ontologically, Father, Son, and Spirit are thus described as nodes in a network of relations. Moreover—and this is the divine difference from created relational structures—these nodes are not antecedent to the relations in which they stand, or indeed in any way independent of them. The divine identities or "persons" are relations founded in themselves, *relationes subsistentes in Deo* (Thomas Aquinas, *Summa theologica* 1.29.4). The important point for our concern is that this sort of analysis is merely a conceptualized appropriation of the just-noted logic of the New Testament's way of speaking about God. Christians speak and so live in a spiritual space shaped

47

by specific coordinates: Father of this Son/Son of this Father/ liberating Spirit of their love. Insofar, the pattern of the creed and the grammar of the New Testament's specific God-discourse are identical.

There is a second way in which the structure of the creed is determined by a central feature of the New Testament. Prayer is the chief act of faith, so that Matthew's and Luke's report of the prayer Jesus taught his disciples (Matt. 6:9–13 and par.) is a key item of their apostolic witness. The prayer's petitions themselves are typical of Jewish piety of the time; only two things are distinctive. One is that the eschatological petitions come first and those for temporal needs second, instead of Jewish prayer's more usual other way around. But for our concern the vital specificity is the prayer's address, to "Our Father."

As has often been observed, while Israel—as notably documented at Isaiah 63:16—and Judaism—with, for that matter, much of antiquity—could indeed think of God as a Father, individuals in Judaism did not claim his paternity in the first-person singular, or presume directly to address him as "my/our Father." Even in the passage from Isaiah, "our Father" is an appellative and not the term of address. Notoriously, Jesus did both, and this point holds even if one wholly distrusts John's Gospel as a provider of historical information. In giving the church the prayer he did, Jesus permitted and invited us to, if one may so speak, piggyback on his relation to the Father and attach our prayer to his address to his Father.

Thus we have the classic pattern of Christian prayer: for most occasions and purposes, Christians pray *to* the one Jesus called Father, *with* Jesus the Son, who has the intrinsic right to do this, and as we thus enter the relation between them, we pray *in* the Spirit, who is that relation of mutual love. When I am asked to explain the Trinity, I often ask, "Do you know how to pray the Lord's Prayer?" If the answer is "Yes," I then reply, "Then you do understand the Trinity."

To grasp how the Apostles' Creed works, it is therefore vital to notice, as is often not done, that not only is the creed patterned by the canonical baptismal mandate's triune name for God and by the triune habit of the New Testament's language, but also by the shape of the New Testament's specific instruction in prayer, by its instruction in how to respond affirmatively to the church's message. We must next observe how that works for each of the three identities.

48

As Christian prayer is normally spoken directly to the Father, so in the creed what follows "I believe in God the Father" is *doxology*: "Almighty, Creator of heaven and earth . . ." If additional doxological predicates for God—as perhaps "All-Knowing" or "All-Merciful" or "Redeemer of the world" or "Sanctifier"—were to be added to the creed, these too would belong in the *first* article.

Since Christian prayer is done together with the Son, so in the creed what follows "and in Jesus Christ" and the claim that this man is "his only Son, our Lord" is recitative appropriation of acts of God by which his Son Jesus is indeed our Lord, so that we are in a position to address God as Father. In abstract principle, a second creedal article could be a summary of the whole Pentateuch, the Gospels, and the book of Revelation.

As Christian prayer is done in the Spirit, so in the creed what follows "and in the Holy Spirit" is specification of what it means for us that we are indeed in the Spirit and so have place before the Father with the Son. Here we acknowledge that this spiritual location is constituted by the church and in fellowship also with the departed saints—for "communion of saints" is certainly not in apposition; that it is established by baptism for the forgiveness of sin; and that it is directed to resurrection into God's eternal life.

Both as the creed is shaped by the triadic baptismal name and as it is shaped to the pattern of Christian prayer, it has a quite different trinitarian structure than is often thought. It is frequently supposed that the Apostles' Creed attributes creation to the Father, redemption to the Son, and sanctification to the Spirit. But the text does not parcel out the triune work in such fashion. For the first article does not in fact tell of the act of creation; rather, it praises the Father with a personal doxological epithet "Creator"—and as we just noticed, the Western creed's first article could for centuries get along even without this. Nor does the third article narrate the course of our sanctification; rather, it acknowledges sanctification's contexts. Narrative belongs in the christological second article. Thus, for example, "Redeemer" as a predicate belongs to the triune God as one God, and so descriptively to all and each of the three; but if it were used in the creed, it would adhere to the Father as the addressee of such doxology; then it is in confessing the Son that the actual story of redemption is told.

49

Insofar, therefore, the shape of the creed and the shape of the canon match. "In the beginning" there is just God, who is always to be praised. Then, as the church reads its Scripture, the whole narrative from Genesis 1:3 through the Old Testament's historical books and the Gospels tells one long christological story, of God's works done, as the New Testament tells us, "in Christ." Finally, the Father is praised in this fashion, and his works in the Son are confessed in this fashion from within a life structured by the self-giving of the Spirit; that is, within a life whose paradigm we see in the remaining parts of both Testaments.

The previous paragraph does, however, begin with "insofar." For the match between canon and creed is not perfect. I have already complained about the way in which the creedal tradition skips over God's history with old Israel. Even within the brevity imposed by the purpose of creeds, there might well have been a clause or two of the sort earlier suggested. Since there are no such clauses, this much at least can be done: churchly instruction in the creed should emphasize how the second article's opening "Christ" and "Lord" derive their meaning from God's history with Israel, and in reciting the creed we should always be aware of this reference.

We may here note also the way in which the creed makes another skip, over the life of Jesus between birth and execution. The apostle Paul is similarly reticent, but the relation of the creed's reticence to that of Paul may never be clarified. We earlier noted the conversely notched fit between creed and canon, and praised it; but this beneficent pattern would not have been much obscured by a creedal clause evoking Jesus' ministry between birth and death. Since there are no such clauses, our recitation and use of the creed must, and inevitably will, involve mental identification of "Jesus Christ" from the story told about him in Scripture.

The point of these last observations: we cannot suppose that the Apostles' Creed, or any other actual creed, is a complete summary of the faith or is by itself an adequate guardian of the church's continuing apostolicity. Churchly declarations sometimes assert that the creed contains everything we need to believe. This is true only if we read the creed in its just-described deference to the canon. We are even more often told that the canon of Scripture contains "all things necessary for our salvation." This is true only if in reading Scripture we let the structure of the creed guide us to Scripture's overall trinitarian structure, and also let the teaching of the creed determine our reading of such biblical phenomena as those discussed in following chapters.

50

PART TWO

Extensions

CHAPTER 6

The Canonical Text

The notion of canon has a secondary use that in current circumstances I cannot simply pass over. In academic theology and in scholarly discourse generally, we sometimes refer to "the canonical text" of a passage of Scripture, or indeed of any work of literature, as distinct from a text that is plainly different but is nevertheless supposed to be somehow a text of the same passage. The "canonical text" of a biblical passage is the one the church proposes as Scripture, to be read in worship, devotion, pedagogy, and so forth. One may say, not quite tautologically or facetiously, that the canonical text of a passage is the one that is found in the canonized book.

Other-than-canonical texts of a biblical passage may be of several sorts. There are passages where some manuscripts show textual variants that probably should not be adopted but are nevertheless too striking to be simply ignored. The ending of Mark poses a problem of somewhat different sort: Is Mark 16:9–20 canonical, or does the canonical text end with the terror of the women? John 7:53–8:11 is a similar case. In these cases, by what standard might choice be justified? No doubt we might identify yet other sorts of "uncanonical" texts.

In this chapter, however, only two, distantly related, questions will concern us. The one is specifically modern: What is the status of the canonical text of a passage over against a scholarly construction that is said to represent an "earlier" or even "original" version of the passage? Or what if any is the role of the latter over against the former? The other is a question posed by the history of Judaism's and the church's use of Scripture: Which version of the Old Testament is in fact the church's canonical text, the Hebrew or the ancient Greek translation called the Septuagint?

The first question is important because in modern exegesis there has been a tendency to regard what we may call ancestor texts as the authentic texts, rather than those found in the writings as canonized. Thus a commentator of one of the prophets, for instance Eichrodt in his standard work on *Ezekiel*, will analyze a passage to identify and sequester editorial glosses and interpolations, additions by the prophet's circle of followers, and so forth, and then treat the remainder as the text to be given serious attention. Or again, form criticism of Jesus' parables, such as the classic work by Jeremias (*Parables*), seeks to backtrack the path of churchly tradition that carried a parable from someone's immediate memory of Jesus' utterance at a particular time and place over the decades to the version textually fixed in a Gospel. The situations and concerns in the Christian community or communities that handed on a parable were of course different from those Jesus himself addressed, and the community's concerns will inevitably have shaped the way the parable was remembered, told, retold, and eventually edited as text. Working back through this history, redaction-critical and form-critical research seeks to reach some approximation of what Jesus himself is likely to have said. Now, if something close to Jesus' own utterance can with any plausibility be discovered, must this not be the text to which followers of Jesus should attend?

So far in this book, I have assumed that the role of the canon in the church's life belongs to the canonical texts. But this is by no means universally acknowledged also by exegetes who intend their work to serve the life of the church. Indeed, scholarly discussion often classifies this assumption as merely one methodological option, "the canonical method," and perhaps denigrates it as narrow or conservative.

Which version of, for example, the parable of the Sower should occupy a sermon, or be the occasion of private meditation, or be initially put forward for discussion in a seminary class? Should it be the canonical text, which presents itself as an allegory of differently amenable soils, and offers a rationale for the church's varying

54

and sometimes disappointing experience with sowing the Word? Or should it be the parable that some critical scholars, and the present author, think Jesus himself probably told: of a bizarrely behaving sower, one so careless and prodigal of his gifts that he scatters them as no sane farmer would—an utterance that directly rebuked those offended by Jesus' reckless self-giving to all sorts and conditions of humanity?

In the case just cited, the parable told by Jesus himself—supposing for the sake of argument that the suggestion above approximates it—is much the more interesting. Why then should it be the canonical text that is read and interpreted in the church? There is a quick answer, which also covers the other genres of Scripture: because it was the existent texts of the Old Testament and of the New Testament writings that imposed themselves on the church as Scripture in the first place. The "canonical text" is the text that was canonized; and therefore it is the text to which the church's exegesis is finally directed.

This answer is not only quick, and indeed close to tautologous; it is also sufficient. For apart from the canon's role as a collection of texts the church assembled to serve its specific needs, the volume comprising the canon is not a plausible literary or historical unit, and no one would be reading it nor would I be writing about it. Apart from the fact that Israel's Scripture funded the initial church, and apart from the fact that the church collected writings of its own in one book with this Scripture, there would have been no "Holy Bible," and there would be no reason to treat the documents now bound together under that title as anything but sundry relics of two or more ancient Mideastern religions. It is only because the church maintains the collection of these documents, with the texts they presented, as the book she needs, that we are concerned for their interpretation.

But though the quick answer seems conclusive, many exegetes, including some committed to the church, are not moved by it. Many also among churchly scholars insist that the Jesus we are to worship and follow must be the "real historical" Jesus, who is to be encountered only by painstaking investigation and reconstruction. Whatever authority the canonical text of the Gospels may have in other contexts, the biblical scholar's work—it is held by such exegetes—must treat the canonical text of the Gospels as a starting point and as a source of clues to its own reconstruction, whether this is then driven by skepticism about the texts or by benevolence toward them.

How are we to understand this attitude? It is important to see that it is occasioned by theologically powerful considerations. I will continue with the Gospels as the case in point. And I will begin from the logical structure of the Gospels, by virtue of which, as I earlier maintained, they offer themselves as Scripture.

A Gospel, I said, is logically a long proposition of the form: "Jesus of Nazareth, the one who . . . and who . . . and who . . . , is risen from the dead." The narrative identification of Jesus that fills the ellipses claims to specify a particular human being, who lived in the time and space inhabited also by Mary of Nazareth and a Roman official named Pontius Pilate and the readers and author of this book. For if the events referred to by the narratives were not supposed to have occurred in our created time and space, they would not specify someone who could suffer a unique feature of our time and space, death, and so could be raised from death. It is necessarily a "historical Jesus" whose death the Gospels can tell and whose resurrection they then can proclaim.

The problem is that this inhabitant of first-century Palestine cannot be entirely identical with the Jesus portrayed in the Gospels, since each of the Gospels narrates some events and reports some discourses differently than do the rest of them, sometimes importantly and irreconcilably. And it often does seem that we can trace the tradition-processes by which these variations have come to pass. Nor do we need to affirm the results of any particular such attempt to make the present point; the mere possibility of the attempt suffices.

Again for example, did the historical Jesus lay down the order of church discipline reported by Matthew (18:15–17)? He may well have mandated mutual rebuke and forgiveness among his disciples, but a formal legal procedure surely seems to be more at home in a later more organized community than in the necessarily somewhat amorphous band following an itinerant rabbi and prophet. And having reasoned so, we can next ask: Given the disciplinary needs for which a congregation or congregations are likely to have queried and so shaped the saying, what remembrance of Jesus' discourse may they have started from?

Such matters are consequential: a believer who says "Jesus is risen" carries at the back of consciousness a narrative sketch of who this Jesus is, a picture that will not be identical with the narrative of any of the Gospels; and this picture shapes the import of ". . . is risen." It would not be good news that "Jesus of Nazareth, who preyed upon his followers, . . . is risen."

Must then the church's exegetes not indeed try to discover the Jesus about whom all the Gospels tell but who is not exactly described by any of their tellings? That is, cannot the church's exegetes seek to uncover a historical Jesus behind the Gospels? They can, and some among them will surely do it, however one may assess the chances of success. Nevertheless, as we started by insisting, the church cannot think that the canonical texts of the Gospels do *not* portray the Jesus who walked and talked "back then." This is the dilemma on both horns of which modern churchly exegesis has been impaled.

It seems to me and to some others that what has been lacking is a distinction that, once noticed, is fairly obvious: we should distinguish "the historical Jesus" from "the historians' Jesus"—thereby, to be sure, departing from most previous uses of the label "historical Jesus." I will here appropriate that label to designate a person who is presumed, rightly or wrongly, to have inhabited our time and space. The label "the historians' Jesus" will then designate the constructs resulting from critical historians' efforts to describe this person. The historical Jesus is the person who had a life in first-century Palestine of our time and world, and just so can have died and just so can be risen. The historians' Jesus is, once one stops to think about it, not a person at all; "the historians' Jesus" can only be a label for a class of documents, the Jesus-historians' remarkably different and indeed often quite incompatible reports of their researches and speculations.

This is not to say that the historians' labors are pointless. Thus the historical Jesus must surely have had a last meal with his disciples. But was this a Passover meal, as the Synoptic Gospels record it? Or did the last communal meal happen on the night before the Passover, as John has it, so that the Last Supper was a more usual communal meal, and so that Jesus died as the Passover lambs were being slain? It is the historians' task to try to determine which account, if either, is more likely to be accurate. And any plausible result of their researches would indeed make a difference in several contexts, including that mostly subliminal sketch of Jesus' life by which, in the daily exercises of faith and theology, believers identify the one who is risen. Indeed, even as the scholarly effort continues to be inconclusive, we all in the ordinary practice of faith, and specifically in liturgy, presume one dating or the other.

Thus "historical-critical method" does have a role in our grasp of the historical Jesus. The point here made is only that its results cannot themselves be supposed to constitute that grasp. Classic liberal theology's elevation of the historians' Jesus to the role of Savior—and therewith implicitly the elevation of "historical-critical" research to be the chief means of grace!—was simply the rather crude category mistake of mistaking a pile of scholarly reports for a person.

So how do we come to know the historical Jesus, the actual inhabitant of created time and space? Let it first be said that we have grounds to claim *any* knowledge of him only if the Spirit indeed guided and guides the church's effort to know him. In itself, this proposition is nothing remarkable; all claims to know something factual about the past, about "how it really was back then," depend on faith in a will that is moving history and on the possibility of our knowing something of that will. For if there is no purpose drawing temporal events onward, then time is simply a plotless one thing after another; and if time is simply one thing after another, each of those things is in turn divisible into a sequence of one thing after another, and so on toward an infinity in which no specific persons or events appear. Only if there is someone who has a purpose for time, so that historical events cohere in a reality other than themselves, is there a coherent and narratable past—a point powerfully made in its negative obverse form by a recent French variety of atheism, which said that just because there is no God, no story can be both coherent in itself and grasp any reality beyond itself. But a historiography that eschews teleological narrative must eventually undo itself altogether—which is the very purpose of these deniers.

On the other hand, if the Spirit does guide the church's witness to what happened back there, then *this* "quest for the historical Jesus" has possibilities beyond those available to the critical historian qua critical historian. A first such: we can receive the fourfold Gospels as a single gift of the Spirit and therefore trust that the witness that the Spirit-led church from time to time draws from the Gospels is reliable knowledge of the historical Jesus, even while some of us keep trying to resolve such questions as the day of the

58

crucifixion. And then a second: we can even be given reliable information about the historical Jesus in altogether different ways than that of the modern historian. I will instance just one such gift.

It is likely that 2 Isaiah's evocation of "a man of sorrows, and acquainted with grief" (Isa. 53:3 KJV), and the church's iconography and hymnody based on the passage, have contributed more to the picture of Jesus that believers carry with them—and so to the import of ". . . is risen"—than most pages of the Gospels. Are the pious therein deluded? Not if the word that came to 2 Isaiah is indeed one person with the historical Jesus, and not if that very Jesus is not now dead but alive to speak in and by the church. For then the church's adopting of Isaiah's verbal picture is nothing less than the historical Jesus' own guidance to a true depiction of himself. In Irenaeus's church, this reasoning would not have seemed remarkable, if indeed anyone would have bothered to urge something so obvious. By the warrants and mandates of modernity's thinking, the claim is certainly bizarre; but if indeed Jesus is what the church claims he is, the one eternal Word of God, there is no reason to be long deterred by secular modernity's inhibitions.

What then, within this broadened and more rational view of historical testimony, is the role of the canonical text of passages from the Gospels? There is a slogan of Reformation theology, that is now ecumenically acceptable: the Scriptures are the "working norm that is subject to no norm," the *norma normans non normata*, of our knowledge of divine things. That is, the Scriptures are not the whole of the church's cognitive heritage; they are the part that trumps and cannot be trumped. Applied to the case of our knowledge of the historical Jesus, the canonical Gospels are the criterion of what can be accepted as indeed Spirit-enabled testimony. The Gospels, and the few other biographical hints in the New Testament, may not be the only informants about the Jesus who inhabited first-century Palestine, but no claim about him that conflicts with them can be authentic.

I have made the relation between the canonical Gospels' portrayal of Jesus and historically reconstructed portrayals of Jesus this chapter's case in point. Mutatis mutandis, analogous analyses could be conducted for other genres of canonical text. We will not embark on the whole project; that would be a book by itself and lead us too far from our central matter. The general rule must be that if we are

59

to know the plain truth propounded by Scripture, then "historical-critical" practices and results cannot stand alone; instead, they must serve understanding of the canonical narrative. The true purpose of tracing the history behind a canonical text, and perhaps of reconstructing ancestor texts along the way of the history, is to help in elucidating the canonical text itself. This is by no means a minor contribution; it may indeed have become more vital in modernity's and late modernity's intellectual climate.

And now perhaps I may be permitted an excursus, which can also serve as an instance of the immediately foregoing. Back a few pages, readers may well have asked: So? How would *you* exegete the parable of the Sower? If the parable "to be read in the churches" is the canonical allegory of hearers' various aptitudes for the gospel, is any contribution made to its interpretation by your guess about Jesus' own saying?

Let me suggest: an informed guess about the original parable, that it was Jesus' direct and personal challenge to those offended by his careless self-sowing, can enforce a vital point also about the canonical text into which it developed, and about the event of that text's public interpretation. When preachers and teachers throw out the Word and, like the sower in the canonical parable, find that they do not control what happens with it, they lack control, I suggest, because also this churchly event is a confrontation with the unpredictably profligate Christ; because, indeed, it is he who is finally doing the sowing. At least two exegetical consequences may be noted.

First, speaking and hearing the Word are exercises at once riskier and more hopeful than usual homiletics and catechetics would lead one to suspect. Thus the exegete of the soils parable is not merely assigned to exhort hearers or readers to be good soil or to scare away the "birds of the air" or do some hoeing and dunging to improve the shallow soil or to perform any other controllable act. Nor is the preacher or teacher simply to lament the bad soil and praise the good soil. Those involved in proclamation of this parable encounter Christ in this act—or better, Christ takes over their act—and where Christ sows, wonders can happen. That possibility must control interpretation of our parable.

60   Second, if the canonical parable is not read with an ear for the transforming presence of Christ, the soils have to be regarded as fixed entities: when the gospel comes along, some hearers are

antecedently of one sort and some are of another; some are antecedently apt to hear the gospel and persevere in it, and others for various reasons are not. Expounding the canonical parable with any integrity, the question of predestination, indeed of double predestination, is thus unavoidable, however much preachers or teachers may wish to avoid it. The more christological and perhaps more historically original version may remind us that the "pre" in predestination does not point to an event before encounter with Christ. For if Christ is who the church says he is, nothing comes before him; all things are created by and for him. The Son is begotten before all time, and the Son and Christ are one person. Rather, eternal predestination happens precisely in the meeting with the eternally living Christ; and telling our parable is itself such a meeting. A faithful sermon on our parable will not be a sermon about predestination; it will be a predestining sermon.

One may even imagine a pastoral dialogue: Seeker: "Am I among the elect?" Pastor: "Yes." Seeker: "How do you know?" Pastor: "You are elect because in Jesus' name I now promise that you are." Seeker: "But it's plain that I am barren soil!" Pastor: "When Christ comes sowing, all things are possible." Seeker: "When will that happen to me?" Pastor: "I just told you. This is it."

We come to our second problem, which we can treat more briefly, if perhaps less satisfactorily. The canonical text is the text that was canonized. But in the case of the Old Testament, what text was that? The Old Testament was indeed mostly written in Hebrew. But the Greek Septuagint—probably made for the Jewish community in Egypt, where Greek was the common language—was extant by the second century before Christ. Thus this Greek Old Testament was in place when Israel's Scripture funded the church, and was in fact the text used by the New Testament tradents and writers. Moreover, for a century, and in the Eastern church for many centuries after that, the Septuagint remained the church's Old Testament for liturgical and scholarly use. Therefore a strong case can be made that the Greek rather than the Hebrew is the church's canonical text, whatever was the case in old Israel.

The picture, however, quickly becomes more ambiguous. The churches in the territories of the Western empire soon needed the Scriptures in *their* common language, which was Latin rather than Greek, and translations began to appear in—that favorite period of ours—the later second century. At first they were apparently made from the Greek. But consciousness that the Greek was itself a translation remained, so that when at the beginning of the fifth century, Jerome undertook the task of finally providing a full, reliable, and semiofficial Latin version, he turned to what he called the "original Hebrew" for all but the Psalter. And for a thousand years Jerome's version, the Vulgate, was the Latin-speaking church's authoritative Old Testament, just as the Septuagint had been. Thus a case might even be made that in the West the Vulgate is the canonical text.

How are we to deal with this? It would seem that at least in the case of the Old Testament, the fixity characteristic of Scripture is not dependent on fixity of language. And indeed, unlike translations of the Qur'an, which must not be titled "The Qur'an" but rather must have such titles as "The Meaning of the Koran," Christian Scripture is inherently translatable; an English version is simply "The Holy Bible."

Let me first propose a bit of theory consonant with this situation, then propose what is more important: practice. My theory can be quickly stated: strictly speaking, the canonical text of the Old Testament is neither the Hebrew nor the Greek by itself, but both texts together and either text if need be. Practice will then depend on the situation with a particular passage. When we can discover reasonable grounds for supposing that one or the other text is "better," by any of the rules usual among textual critics, that is the canonical text. When this is not possible, we should refuse to choose and interpret both.

But how can the fixity definitive of a Scripture be independent of fixity of language? It is possible only if we again trust the Spirit. We must trust the purposes of the Spirit both in the history that leads to the dual text, and in the problem with which he thus leave us.

CHAPTER 7

Dogma

We devoted the previous chapter to the notion of "canonical text," as an extension to the main discussion of canon. The topic of creed also, I think, demands an attachment; I must discuss the matter of "dogma." For in its own way dogma reprises the original creedal development and participates in its authority; this chapter will treat what that way may be. By "dogma" we will in the following denote binding teaching that emerges after the establishment of stable baptismal creeds, postcreedal but nevertheless binding doctrine. If this restricted usage of the word "dogma" seems idiosyncratic to this book, I ask readers simply to bear with the stipulation.

The problems that occasioned the emergence of the canon and the creedal tradition were far from the last of that sort that the church would encounter. The second-century appearance of the telephone-game problem was only the first of many. The mission—the mandate for one person to tell another person about the resurrection, who is to tell yet another, and so on—is constitutive of the church; indeed, the pursuit of the mission and the perdurance of the church come to the same thing. Therefore the church is continually driven to cross geographical and temporal boundaries; for it, the harvest is always whiter on the other side of some cultural or historical fence. And beyond each fence new questions wait.

In obedience to its mandate, the church immediately began to transgress geographic fences, moving from Judea and Galilee northward and westward into the general Hellenistic civilization of late Mediterranean antiquity, and eastward into Mesopotamia and Persia and the multiple cultures between Persia and India. Such movement has never ceased; indeed, it sometimes laps itself, as when missioners from Europe and North America returned to Middle Eastern territories that once were demographic heartlands of Christianity, until they were ground down by Islamic conquest and rule.

The peoples of the western Mediterranean littoral—or of Persia, or of northern Europe or of southern Africa or of China or . . . —were not and are not blank slates when the gospel arrives. Each new cultural turf has its own antecedent gods, each its own corresponding construal of reality, each its thereby established and perhaps well-reasoned morality. Therefore, when someone arrives to say that Jesus of Nazareth is risen and why this is great news, each has also its own questions and difficulties. For an early and archetypical example, when in Luke's account Paul proclaimed the resurrection—in Greek, *anastasis*—in Athens (Acts 17:15–32), it seems that all the Athenian elite could make of this, within their existing construal of reality, was that he must be promoting a new fertility goddess named Anastasis. They could fit the fertility gods' eternal cycle of life and death into their understanding of reality, as a symbolic representation of the deep timelessness of ultimate reality. But an actual resurrection, a permanent conquest of death? Where would that leave us?

Among temporal boundaries that the church has surmounted, we may instance the fourth- and fifth-century collapse of the Roman order in which the church had grown and had found its precarious place. In large stretches of Western Europe, the church suddenly found itself the chief still-functioning communal institution, and out of sheer care for the neighbor it became responsible for preserving minimal social order. Thus a sixth-century pope, Gregory called the Great, never finished his scholarly labors on Ezekiel because he repeatedly had to break off and negotiate with Lombard raiders at Rome's gates, there being no one else to do it. The Eastern empire continued until the fifteenth century, but there also the church was drafted to provide otherwise lacking ideological and moral coherence, in the process becoming a state religion with all the power and temptations of that role. How a community whose home is in a kingdom not of this age, and that within this age was

64

formed as a persecuted minority, was to manage such assignments was a theological problem that agitated the church for centuries. Indeed, in its negative form it still does: for example, how are the still legally established but drastically diminished churches of Scandinavia or Britain to comport themselves over against other public institutions? Can Westminster Abbey remain both Christian and a symbol of state sovereignty, when most citizens are unbelieving or Muslim?

After a major historical turning point, a society does not necessarily continue in its old construal of reality or its old morality. If anything, the new questions that the church confronts after a temporal break in a familiar society may be more challenging than those that it encounters in a newly invaded society. Thus the churches of northern Europe and North America have yet to master spiritually or conceptually the suddenly revealed nihilistic impetus of late Western modernity. What, for example, does marriage mean in a society that values all sexual acts solely by the personal benefits they provide the pair? As it becomes plain that the surrounding culture accepts and indeed promotes "marriages" that are not constituted by the scriptural mandate of permanent union between male and female, the church must ask: Why exactly are unions that *are* constituted by that mandate entitled to the special recognition that the church presumes? And indeed, how shall the church preserve their place even in its own community? The old maxims are plainly not up to the challenge, and the replacements now being put into place are even less so.

The need for theological hard thinking is thus a permanent feature of the church's life as it repeatedly enters new cultures and new epochs within familiar cultures. And sometimes the results of such reflection become permanently authoritative in the church's life. Thus arises a body of theologoumena that have a role closely analogous to that of creedal statements; it is these that I here, perhaps oddly, call "dogma."

Such dogma differs from creed in that it does not directly emerge from the community's founding communal consensus, the *regula fidei*. For dogma responds to questions that did not arise in the second- or third-century church, and to which the *regula fidei* and the creeds may not supply obvious answers. But if dogma cannot always be supported by direct appeals to the church's initial communal certainty, what *does* support it?

As the contingencies of history provide, we can see the actual transition from creed to dogma in the history and text of the Nicene Creed. We must first sketch the theological crisis that precipitated its writing (further to this, see Jenson, *Theology*, 1:90–114).

By 300 or so, most bishops and other theologians, at least in the East where the intellectual action was, were in one or another degree conceptually inspired by the writings of the great Origen of Alexandria, from the previous century. The conflict that broke out was between parties who took their Origenism at different strengths.

Origen's trinitarian theology was what historians of doctrine call "subordinationist": it conceived of the Son and the Spirit as making a structure of mediating steps down from the Father to created beings, thus ordering them "under" the Father. From around the middle of the second century, as I earlier noted, much of the church's intellectual life was dominated by Gentiles whose education had been in the thought of the Greek pre-Christian theologians. For Plato, Aristotle, and their epigones, it was a defining character of deity that it is "impassible," unaffected by the vicissitudes of temporal history; the Scriptures, on the other hand, depict a God deeply affected by his people's struggles, an involvement that culminated in God the Son's very earthly passibility on the cross. Theologians from Justin the Martyr through Origen managed the dissonance by locating the Son a tiny ontological step down from the Father himself, so that the Son, as not *quite* so divine as the Father, could do the suffering while the Father maintained the divine immunity.

But subordinating the Son to the Father in this fashion posed a dangerous question: Is the Son then really God in the same way as is the Father, or does he lodge somewhere *between* the Creator and the creatures? And if the Origenist consensus suggests the latter view, do the Scriptures countenance such a middle realm between Creator and creature? Most theologians finessed the question, until early in the fourth century a not very subtle Alexandrian priest named Arius said plainly and aggressively that to suffer for us, God the Son must be less God than God the Father. His bishop deposed him for downgrading the Son; some other bishops thought there must be at least a spark of Origenist truth in Arius's position and came to his defense; and the existing consensus disintegrated.

The dilemma that subordinationism had always posed was starkly revealed: If the Son is not quite fully God, how can we worship him? If he is fully God, how can he suffer for us? People found themselves pushed to one side or the other of the apparent dilemma, and each party saw in the position of the other a deadly threat to Christian faith: some feared the loss of a divine Savior, and others feared the loss of a suffering Savior.

In 325 the church's first general gathering of bishops assembled at Nicaea to deal with the threatening collapse of church unity— which, we may note, happened anyway. After long debate the bishops decided against Arius. It was perhaps not so clear what they decided *for*.

It is not the content of the bishops' decision or its consequences that we are here principally concerned with, but with the way history presented them with a problem that their creedal commitments did not contemplate, and with their procedure in dealing with it. They took an available catechetical/baptismal creed as a starting point, then formulated their theological decisions by interpolating it, inserting among other phrases "true God from true God," "begotten, not made," and most notably the more-or-less technical phrase "of one substance/reality/being with the Father," *homoousion tō patri*. The resulting creed was confirmed by a second council, at Constantinople in 381, which then issued its own closely similar creed with additions to cover other matters, the present Niceno-Constantinopolitan creed.

The Niceno-Constantinopolitan procedure, meeting new questions by expanding the creed, did not prove workable. Baptismal candidates do not really need to know such things as what the pseudo-philosophical word *homoousios* might mean; indeed, most of the bishops at Nicaea seem to have had no clue, other than that Arius had once objected to it. And the creed they interpolated was mostly about other matters than those the bishops had come together to deal with. Moreover, the contending parties after Nicaea took to laying out their positions by imitating Nicaea and each writing its own creed, thus undoing the function of creeds. A council at Chalcedon in 451 prohibited the further writing of creeds and stated its own decisions as a set of semilegal mandates: "We teach. . . ." This more direct procedure became standard.

So why should anyone believe that, for example, the Son is "begotten, not made"? One can argue that the Nicene formulations merely package what the Scriptures say about the Son—and that seems to me to be plainly the case. But it remains that also the Arians and post-Nicene almost-Arians and super-Arians could and did quote Scripture by the page. As for the creedal tradition, the Arians argued that language like "who was made as the first and pattern of all creatures," à la Proverbs' personal Wisdom (Prov. 8), would fit perfectly well after "his only Son, our Lord"—though again I think this mistaken.

The point is not that the Nicene formulas are not demanded by Scripture, but that one could think that they are not without manifestly departing from what had until Nicaea been accepted as the standard of true teaching. To affirm Nicaea's dogma with a certainty analogous to that appropriate to the rule of faith and the catechetical/baptismal creeds, we have to posit another source of assurance to go with the creed and Scripture. And the only thing available is an authority of the council itself.

That is to say, we must trust that the Spirit guided the council, that one can put in the bishops' mouths the formula with which the so-called apostolic council proclaimed its decisions: "It has seemed good to the Holy Spirit and to us" (Acts 15:28). Generalizing, dogma rests on Scripture and creed *and* on what is now called the magisterium, an institution in the continuing life of the church that is credited with Spirit-led authority to discern the underlying scriptural and creedal truth.

There is, to be sure, no ecumenical agreement about where such a teaching authority might be located. Most Christians agree that ecumenical councils on the pattern of Nicaea can proclaim dogma. But how many such councils have there been? And could there be new ones? One generally speaks of seven "ecumenical councils." But Roman Catholic lists include several more; these are regarded by the rest of the ecumene as, though in themselves perhaps exemplary, merely provincial Roman synods. The Roman Catholic Church holds also that the bishop of Rome, by virtue of his place as head and representative of the body of bishops, can at need proclaim dogma with or without an assembled council; this too is doubted by most other Christians. Until quite recently, the Reformation churches treated their theological faculties as magisterial, with decidedly mixed results. And finally on this list of dissents, some Protestants altogether reject the notion of a distinct institutional magisterium, locating teaching authority in the local congregation or even in the individual believer.

Assuming the majority position, how is it that we can we trust conciliar dogma? In a famous debate at Leipzig, Martin Luther was driven to say that "a council can err"; this was seized as proof that he was a dangerous schismatic. Yet Luther did not think that any of the ecumenically accepted councils had actually erred or indeed could have erred. His actual view seems to have been something like this: if the teaching of a reputed council can be shown to be contrary to Scripture or creed, it would just thereby be discovered not to be a real council. We encounter yet again the circularity that marks the work of the Spirit.

With the rule of faith or the baptismal creeds, no division is possible between their formal character and the truth of what they affirm. But with dogma there is a disjunct between the formal character of a body that purports to lay down dogma and the truth of what they lay down: a doctrine may be proclaimed in a way seemingly marked by every formality of proper authority and still not be true to the church's message. Thus a council held at Ephesus in 449 was established in what then was a usual way yet is nevertheless known as the "robber council" because it did not teach what two years later, at a council in the same city, was found to be the true doctrine. Or again, a seventh-century pope, Honorius I, whom no one regards as a false pope, issued a formal endorsement of "monothelitism"—about which I will later have something to say—but was reversed by his successor and then by a council. The pope, according to Catholic conviction, is doctrinally infallible when he speaks ex cathedra, that is, specifically and directly in his role as ecumenical pastor. That Honorius was later found to have decreed wrongly in the monothelite matter only proves that he was not speaking ex cathedra.

I do not instance such circularities to denigrate dogma, but to show its dependence on the continuing work of the Spirit. That we treat dogma as almost creedal is a venture, undertaken by faith that the Spirit will not let the church err fatally or in the long term—but just so is indeed a risk, an aspect of the church's communal venture of faith. And if indeed we doubt or defend a dogma, our recourse must be to a *norma normans*, canon and creed together.

69

CHAPTER 8

Episcopacy

In response to the crises of the second century, the church received a trio of institutions to guard its identity through time: canon, creed, and episcopate. In the introduction I expressed guilty relief that the third leg was omitted from my task; there were enough difficult matters to coordinate without the many clustered around this one. And I will not give episcopacy and its emergence the attention given to canon and creed. Nevertheless, a brief mention of episcopacy is unavoidable.

The previous chapter shows why this is so: it was impossible to speak of the church's necessary magisterium without regularly mentioning the bishops. The ecumenical councils were all councils of bishops. Synods and provincial councils of the Eastern churches, the Roman Catholic Church, and the Anglican churches are still councils of bishops; and these bodies together embrace the vast majority of the baptized. As for the claim that the pope has a unique magisterium, however one may regard the claim, it rests on the pope's position as bishop of the church at Rome and resulting leadership of the whole body of bishops. There may be other ways in which a church may have a functioning magisterium, and the present author supposes that there are, but most Christians look to bishops for that necessary blessing.

Until early in the second century, only the apostles themselves were generally recognized as having final authority to propound the true teaching. Beyond that, the initial church's various regions and missionary groupings seem to have had no uniform pattern of pastoral authority. Churches founded by Paul were led—if even "led" is not too assertive a word in this case—by all manner of charismatic ministries. Some churches founded by other apostles and missionaries seem to have had more definite organization from the first, though we can only guess what explicit offices may have been in place. It has even been suggested that in the original congregation at Jerusalem a caliphate was developing around the person of the Lord's brother James. In the Pastoral Epistles we hear of "bishops" and "presbyters"—that is, "elders"—but cannot be sure whether these terms denote different offices or are different names for the same office.

On the other hand, the *role* of the Pastoral Epistles' bishops/presbyters is clear: they are to guard the identity of the congregation's faith with that taught by the apostles—which of course suggests a postapostolic date for the writings (on the exegesis of the relevant passages, see Lips, *Glaube*, 106–61). If now we consider that *episkopos* means "overseer," and that the ruling image was that of a shepherd who watches over his flock to keep it together, we may say that the task of the Pastorals' bishops/presbyters was to guard the simultaneously diachronic and synchronic unity of the churches in their care. The doctrinal magisterium of the Pastorals' bishops/presbyters is then an aspect of this general role: it belongs to their responsibility for unity to prevent or heal disunity in teaching, by discerning what is faithful to apostolic teaching and what is not. And, to recur yet again to Bishop Irenaeus, in *Against Heresies* we see him doing just that.

What we more specifically think of as episcopal governance—the "monarchical episcopate," as historians refer to it—is first documented in the letters of Ignatius of Antioch, written during a long journey to martyrdom, sometime between 105 and 110. Ignatius's vision of the local church and its ministerial structure is perhaps something between description of what actually obtained in his locality and evocation of an ideal. The offices of bishop and presbyter are distinct, and the magisterium belongs to the bishop. In each community where there are Christians, there is to be one local church. Each such church is to be led by a single—hence "monarchical"—bishop, surrounded by a college of presbyters. Only the bishop has the magisterium because only he presides at the Eucharist, where the people gather as one body in Christ and are instructed in the one faith by the one bishop's preaching. This vision of the one bishop at the altar, surrounded by the one body of presbyters, and surrounded again by the one body of the faithful, with the whole structure oriented to unity as the one body of Christ, has remained through history the ideal vision of the bishop's role.

We do not know when or where the monarchical episcopate first emerged or how widely it or this construal of its authority were in place by Ignatius's time. But sometime within the next forty years, monarchical episcopacy became the general pattern of governance.

Thus monarchical episcopacy may be initially regarded as a simple, indeed rather elementary, pattern of churchly governance. As such, it can and does replicate itself at various levels of the church's reality: if there are regional churches, these too will need overseeing shepherds; and if there is one universal church, this too, in the conviction of most Christians, should have its bishop. Indeed, the pattern appears also among groups who claim to have no "bishops" at all; for in fact the local congregations of such groups regularly have one chief pastor—"pastor," we should remember, is Latin for "shepherd"—and a surrounding group of other spiritual leaders.

There is, however, a further and defining feature of the ancient episcopal office: "succession." Irenaeus labored to establish the identity of the gospel as taught in his church with the gospel proclaimed by the apostles. Some of his expressions may suggest that he could do this simply by comparing the content of his teaching with that documented in Scripture. But Irenaeus, as we noted earlier, did not in fact think that this sufficed. He thought that as the teacher of apostolic faith, he personally had to be apostolic in his office.

The church is a community extended through time and space, embracing epochs and cultures in what Paul could call "one body." In the introduction, we asked what sort of community this one body is, and we proposed that it is at least the community of a message. In Irenaeus's view and that of the ancient church generally, this meant that the overseeing teachers of the message—within the concern of the previous chapter, those who carried the magisterium—had themselves to make a corresponding communal body within the body of the church. In Irenaeus's self-understanding, he was not

73

simply the pastor at a particular time of the particular church at Lyon; he could be a bishop only as a member of a fellowship and succession of the bishops. And just as believers are taken into the community of faith by those already in it, so a bishop is taken into a temporally and geographically extended community of bishops by those already in it.

The church brings new members into its community by a rite of baptism. Given the analogy of the community of bishops to the community of the church, we might expect that the community of bishops would have something similar. And indeed in the Pastoral Epistles we see a rite well adapted to that purpose. Timothy is exhorted to practice the "charism" that was given to him, communicated "by prophecy, with the presbytery's laying-on of hands" (1 Tim. 4:14, my trans.). In the Pastorals, a "charism" is a gift of the Spirit for building up the body of the church, as in the letters more certainly attributable to Paul; but it is no longer as there an unpredictable and only spiritually verifiable endowment. At least in the church entrusted to Timothy, the charism in question has become an office: an oddly Spirit-given and Spirit-carried office to be sure, but still an office. It is given by audible and intelligible "prophecy"—that is, Spirit-carried and Spirit-filled utterance—spoken by the presbyters and by the visible laying on of their hands.

To what extent this rite may be regarded as mandatory for the making of bishops or analogous pastoral leaders, in the subsequent life of the church, is disputed in the ecumene. But again, most Christians have thought that it is mandatory, that bishops or pastors are to be taken into the diachronic body of shepherds by a rite of the sort that consecrated Timothy. We may observe that this rite actually mimics the penultimate act of baptism as anciently conducted: prayer for the gifts of the Spirit with imposition of hands.

If the local bishop was to oversee the teaching in his church, he had to look to the teaching in other churches, for also in antiquity people moved around. If someone came to a town and asked to join the Eucharist of the local church, the bishop needed to determine if the candidate was indeed one with the local church's teaching— he might be one of those gnostics. And the best way to be sure was, and is, by knowing what was taught in the church from which the applicant came. Thus very quickly the bishops came to exercise a joint oversight over one another's teaching, and thus over the teach-ing of the universal church. By at latest the middle of the third century, the bishops constituted a collegial magisterium. It was this body that appeared in the ancient councils.

To be sure, the Ignatian vision quickly blurred as local churches grew too large or too spread out for the bishop's people regularly to gather around him for Eucharist. Subsidiary congregations were quite early established, and the presbyters became their usual eucharistic celebrants. Thus where Christianity is or once was popular, it has long been mostly in theory that bishops oversee the one body of their faithful. Functionally, most bishops are shepherds not of the flock but of the presbyters, who do most of the actual shepherding—where, indeed, the bishops have not become pure administrators who shepherd nobody. Nevertheless, in episcopally governed communions the bishops continue to exercise the colle-gial magisterium; and it can be argued that such events as Vatican Council II in the previous century show that the charism evoked in the Pastorals has not been withdrawn.

What then of communions that have no bishops in succession, intentionally or by historical happenstance? The Roman Catholic and Orthodox churches must regard them as deeply "wounded" in their being as churches, to use a term from official Roman Catholic documents. A more Protestant judgment might be that the ques-tion is whether the Presbyterians or the nonepiscopal Lutherans or the Methodists or whoever have other continuing institutions of oversight, exercising a functioning magisterium.

Here it is not my role to promote either judgment. But empiri-cally—harking back to the laments of the introduction—it is plain that the churches of denominational or territorial Protestant-ism now have no very prestigious magisterium, and are governed in a way that barely suffices to maintain an outward and superficial unity of faith. On the other hand, the record of episcopal gover-nance during some periods, including the present moment, may well dampen enthusiasm for its restoration where it is not currently in place.

Finally, one aspect of the traditional construal of episcopacy seems applicable also to other structures of churchly oversight: per-sons must be established in magisterial offices by an act of the sort described in the case of Timothy. Many Christians will call this a "sacrament": a rite that actually gives what it talks about. For no one should claim to speak with the church's authority to whom the Spirit has not given the charism of doctrinal discernment. Nor can anyone claim this gift for oneself; it can only be given by the Spirit's agency in an act of the church. Nor yet can this gift be privately or invisibly given, for the community must know of the gift. Whatever locations the magisterium may occupy from time to time or communion to communion, the charism and a bestowing rite of pastoral oversight must pertain also to these.

PART THREE

Creed/Dogma and Scriptural Exegesis

CHAPTER 9

The Creed as Critical
Theory for Scripture

Luke tells us that the Spirit once brought "Philip the evangelist," one of "the seven" (Acts 21:8), to a traveling Ethiopian official. When Philip came up to the official's carriage, he "heard him reading the prophet Isaiah. [Philip] asked, 'Do you understand what you are reading?' He replied, 'How can I, unless someone guides me?'" (8:30–31). It is not a novel late-modern insight that texts by themselves do not necessarily flaunt the sense they harbor.

A few decades ago, one might have entitled this chapter "The Creed as Hermeneutical Principle." But that phrase now has a somewhat dusty feel, and more contemporary jargon offers an alternative and interesting notion, if we allow ourselves some liberty in appropriating it. I will try the experiment of describing the creed as the "critical theory" appropriate for reading the Scripture.

"Critique" in the here relevant late-modern sense is the attempt to discern what a text "really" imports, as against what it may be taken to say by those not clued in to the text's underlying agenda, as the Ethiopian was not for 2 Isaiah. This exegetical use of the notion of critique has its background in a more general tradition of Western modernity, which I will briefly sketch, in part to suggest why one might want to make this experiment.

Modernity had many births. One was when Copernicus asked a question of a peculiar sort: It surely appears that the sun moves round the earth, but does it really? The seventeenth-century explosion of what we now call "modern science" was enabled by several developments, but one decisive innovation was a deliberate policy of asking such questions, a methodological suspicion that the appearances of things are a screen behind which reality hides itself. At the turn of the seventeenth century, Francis Bacon defined science as "putting nature to the question"—that is, torturing it as though with the rack and hot irons—to make it abandon evasive appearances and yield up its truth; and modernity defined itself by enthusiasm for the project. Through the seventeenth and eighteenth centuries, leading minds of the West worked to extend the range of the "critique of appearances," by the end of the eighteenth century elevating it to be a universal principle of thought; in this respect Immanuel Kant is the great concluding figure.

Applied to the interpretation of texts, the suspicion of appearances becomes suspicion of what a text initially appears to say. Two special features of the critique of *textual* appearances must be noted. First, with texts, what constitutes the deceptive appearances can and does change as the texts are passed down through history. A particular generation may even deliberately construct screening barriers around some set of texts. We will need to attend to this point especially when we come to the New Testament. Second, since texts have authors and/or tradents, the attempt to discern an underlying reality becomes the attempt to discern what these persons really are doing with a writing, what their "agenda" is. The interpretive question becomes "Who is up to what with this piece of writing?"

A named critical theory—"postcolonial theory" or "womanist theory" or whatever—is a particular set of instructions for achieving such insight. As indicated by the adjectives in the various theories' names, such a theory supposes that the underlying agenda of some range of texts is fully visible only to a specifically suspicious eye, peering from its point of view. Thus the full question is not only "Who is up to what with this text?" but also "Who is up to what that we—empathizers with the colonized or black women or—are the ones in position to discern?" Accordingly, any particular critical theory is critique also of viewpoints other than its own—sometimes the viewpoints of other critical theories—from which, it claims, only appearances will be visible.

To be sure, if the theorist is really up to "postmodernist" date, critique turns against its own goal, becoming suspicion that nothing at all underlies discourse, not even someone's nefarious agenda. The text will thus be supposed to be constituted entirely by apparent meanings and to have no unique bearing on reality; interpreters are accordingly directed to find in the text whatever interest they antecedently want to denounce or, much more rarely, praise. Indeed, such critique unmasks the question about what a text truly says as itself the last great appearance, and interpreters are therefore free themselves to be up to whatever they want with the text. How shall I interpret the text? As appearances hiding whatever agenda my own agenda demands that it be hiding.

The church cannot simply opt out of modernity's critical pathos; we may not be of the world, but we are in it, and all in it now are critics. The question has to be "Following *what* critical theory, and penetrating to *whose* agenda, should the church read its Scripture?" My answer is implicit in all the foregoing chapters. The community positioned to perceive what a scriptural text is truly up to is the church, and the creed is the set of instructions for discerning this agenda. The needed suspicious eye is the eye trained in the church to distrust all human religiosity, also as it may appear in Scripture. I cannot systematically develop Christianity's critique of religion here, but aspects of it will appear in the following chapters. And it is the triune God who is up to something with these texts, whose agenda is to be discovered, to be affirmed by the church and denounced by others.

The invocation of God in this context will of course provoke objections. But simply that we adduce God is not legitimately among them. Indeed, acknowledging God, consciously or not, is now necessary for any but the nihilistic critique last described, hard though this still may be for most exegetes to acknowledge. Late-modern extremity, from Nietzsche onward, has cleared away the mediating possibilities, to pose a stark choice. At least in the West, when we read Scripture, or indeed anything but mathematics and formal logic—and some theorists were suspicious even here—either we will, however unknowingly, posit God, or we will lapse into the nihilism just described, in which texts have no definite meaning.

The triune Creator, in this context the Source of being who is also the Word about being, is in person the metaphysical bond between determinate reality and discourse. If there is no such God, then, at least for all we can know, there is no such bond, and texts float free in a void of reference; should there nevertheless be in fact something beyond language, it is out of our reach. Who then says that the text does not say what I want it to say? You, my equally finite fellow interpreter? If there is no triune God, then the professor who tells his class that the text, whether of Scripture or of Shakespeare, means such and such because he says it does, is simply inhabiting the actual situation.

In the church, the nihilist option is not open. Believers in the triune God suppose that because the Creator and his Word are one God, reality and language can meet within this God's creation; and they moreover claim that they can perceive this God's agenda. But how do we do the latter? The answer here proposed is in no way original: we know God's agenda because we know him personally; we can see from his viewpoint because we are personally joined with him. We know him personally in the same way we know one another personally, and we share his vision in the same way we sometimes share one another's vision: by together living through a joint history, in this case the christological history of God with his people. For the story told in Scripture is not about a different people of God than that to which believers now belong, also as interpreters of Scripture. And just as do the members of any temporally extended community, believers have their identities in that history, which they inhabit by memory of its past and anticipation of its future.

What then would be the actual procedure of what might be called a "creedal critical theory" for the reading of Scripture? A recent and in my opinion ground-breaking study of Augustine's exegesis provides a label for what is here proposed: we should seek to discern a "christological plain sense" (Byassee, *Praise*, 205–19). For indeed, Christ—as the creed tells us—is God's agenda in Scripture, and it is God whom we should always try to discern, as what the text before us "really" imports.

We should suppose that both the creed's christological-trinitarian doctrine and the canonical text of Scripture are true; and that both are true in the ordinary-language sense of "true," which does not mean we should not reckon with modalities of ordinary language corresponding to different genres of discourse. Our exegetical question then is "On these suppositions, what must the text before us say, just as it stands on the page?" I call the results of such questioning a christological "plain" sense, since we are not imposing anything on the text, nor will we read figuratively except when this plain sense itself mandates it.

Seeking a christological plain sense will work differently with the two Testaments. As usual in this book, we will first consider the Old Testament. In the nature of the case, we will also have to spend most of the rest of this chapter on it. And we will come at the matter somewhat obliquely.

The old rabbis discerned a single phenomenon in several sorts of scriptural narrative and called it the "Shekinah": God as he inhabits and acts within the history of which he is simultaneously the Creator. The famous rabbinical passage that is always quoted is more drastically trinitarian than many Christians would dare: "Israel (will even say) to God: 'You have redeemed *yourself*. . . .' (For) whenever Israel was exiled, the *Shekinah* went with them into exile. . . . And when at the end of days they return, the *Shekinah* will return with them" (Thoma, *Theology*, 312).

Thus "the Angel of the LORD," who appears so regularly in the Pentateuchal narrative and the Deuteronomic History, is on his appearing invariably identified as a messenger *from* the Lord, a reality distinguished from the Lord by the construct or genitive construction that makes his name: he is precisely the angel *of* the Lord. Yet as each such narrative continues, the Angel turns out to speak and act not *for* the Lord, but *as* the Lord, and indeed is rightly worshiped as the Lord (e.g., Gen. 21:17–19; 22:11–12; Exod. 3:2–4; spectacularly, Judg. 13:2–22). The same Shekinah phenomenon, of a historical agent related *to* the Lord, who simultaneously *is* the Lord, appears also in Old Testament narratives about "the Glory of the LORD" (as in 1 Kgs. 8:10–13) or "the Name of the LORD" (as in Deut. 12:5–11).

One body of such narrative was perhaps most central to Israel's theological experience and provided the rabbis with their name for the common phenomenon they perceived in the Angel of the Lord, the Glory of the Lord, and so forth. In the stories of Israel's wilderness journey, the Angel of the Lord duly appears, in the cloud and the pillar of fire (Exod. 23:20–23). But the Tabernacle was subtly different: it was the *mishkan*, the place of the Lord's "settlement," where he *dwelt* among them. For the settlement itself, the rabbis took a word from the same root. After the building of the temple, its

Most Holy Place became the abiding place of the Shekinah, of the Lord's usually but not always invisible presence above the cherubim-throne. So, was God in heaven or was he in the tent and then later in the temple? To be faithful to the texts, we must say that he was both: he was the one God as God ruling over his people's history from beyond it, and he was the same one God as one who in that history is himself one of its dramatis personae.

Until the church's modern loss of exegetical nerve, it was the church's conviction that these Old Testament narratives display what Christian trinitarianism calls the "second identity" or "second person" of God: the Son who is at once another than the Father and the same God as the Father. The rabbis' perception and the pre-modern church's perception are thus very much in accord—until we come to the Christian claim that this jointly celebrated Presence is now personally available as the man Jesus.

The divergence reveals a step of Christian doctrine yet to be taken. We may take this step by considering one of the most famous and theologically revealing passages in the Old Testament: the vision granted the priest Ezekiel, as the context of his call to prophesy. Ezekiel was shown the heavenly prototype of the temple's cherubim-throne (Ezek. 1:4–28). And on the throne, as the source of the glory that constituted it, was an "appearance" that was "the figure of a man" (1:26, my trans.).

Plainly we have here a very special appearance of the Shekinah, the second identity of God, God as himself a figure in the story he writes. But why does this second identity of God, revealed as occupant of the heavenly throne, look like a man? Classic Christian interpretation has answered, "Because the second triune identity *is* a man, Jesus of Nazareth." This stark proposition offends all normal religiosity, which at this point will want to talk about metaphors or symbols or figures; it is nonetheless a defining theological affirmation of Christianity.

Thus the aforementioned sixth-century Pope, Gregory the Great, expounding Ezekiel, simply presumes that the one above the throne is the man Jesus and concerns himself rather to lay out this man's ontological status: "We should observe how the order is maintained: above the living beings is the firmament, above the firmament is the throne, and above the throne a man is delineated. For above holy men still living in . . . the body are the angels, and above the angels are superior angelic powers closer to God, and above the powers is . . . the man Christ Jesus" (Gregory, *Homilies on Ezekiel*, VIII.20.20–27).

Behind Gregory's presumption is the church's doctrine that the second triune identity and the man Jesus of Nazareth are but one person. As the Apostles' Creed presents the matter, "Jesus" and the Father's "only Son" make a single subject of the following narrative of salvific events. In telling the story of God's acts, there is no way to speak of God the Son that does not refer to the man Jesus, and no way to speak of Jesus that does not refer to God the Son. Such doctrine is funded by the exegetical observation that there is but one Protagonist of the story told by the Gospels, whether he does human things like being born in a womb, or divine things like forgiving sins.

Now if this doctrine is true, then the man on the throne who shines with God's own glory, who indeed *is* God's Glory, must either be Jesus the Christ or something highly problematic. For if the man on the throne is no actual man, but a symbol or picture or something of the sort, then Ezekiel's vision, and most of the Old Testament's other representations of God, are indeed "anthropomorphic," presenting the Shekinah as if he were a man though he is not, and so are relics of ancient paganism, to be at best explained away—as much modern theology has presumed.

What the disciples saw as the "transfiguration" (Mark 9:2–7) tells us which possibility to affirm: there is indeed an actual man who shines with God's own glory and who therefore can have shown himself above the cherubim-throne. The outcome: Christian theology could gloss John 1:1–14 as "In the beginning was the Shekinah, and the Shekinah was with God, and the Shekinah was God. . . . And the Shekinah became flesh and dwelt [*eskēnōsen!*] among us" (RSV alt.). And more important for our assignment, vice versa: the Lord's appearances throughout the Old Testament, as a persona within the very history of which he is the author, are appearances—as the old exegetes put it—"in the person of" the second triune identity, who is Jesus the Christ. Acknowledging this fact will shape how we read every passage of the Old Testament, precisely in its plain sense.

The New Testament is a different matter. For to discover a "christological plain sense" in its texts would seem to require little critical effort, and indeed we will need fewer words on the matter. The Gospels are plainly collections of Christ's remembered words and deeds, and the letters were plainly written to answer questions about him. But here we must remember what we noted earlier: with texts and their tradition, what constitutes "the appearances" varies with history.

As usual, history is a master of irony, for in modernity it has often been critical study itself that has created appearances hiding God's agenda with the New Testament. It is this situation that Karl Barth evoked with his famous remark that the historical-critical exegetes were "not critical enough" for him. Instead of penetrating to the New Testament's underlying agenda, in his judgment they were busily making constructions that turn out to conceal it.

The one great block of the New Testament is the Gospels. Let it be a given: they do not always agree in their narratives of Jesus' words and deeds and sufferings. The historical-critical enterprise has rightly recognized this but then fastened on it, obsessively asking: "What is Matthew's agenda, with his rearrangements of Mark? What is Mark up to, creating a 'Gospel' in the first place? What is Luke's agenda, with his two volumes? And as for John . . . !" It is not that such questions are not legitimate and even in some contexts useful. But the question "What are the Gospels up to with their story of Jesus?" or indeed "What is God up to with the Gospels' story?" has in much modern study disappeared behind the critical questions—and this has sometimes been the deliberate intent. Is there only "Mark's Jesus" or "Matthew's Jesus" or "John's Jesus" and no such thing as simply "the New Testament's Jesus" to be the subject of ". . . is risen"? If there is not, the church's message must be dangerously if not fatally equivocal; if there is, acquaintance with this person must be the final goal of the church's critical reading of the Gospels.

Nor do the apostolic witnesses collected in the New Testament have all the same theology. One may ask why we would expect or want them to. The church's theological tradition has always been less the transfer of a neat body of thought than a continuing discussion, or indeed continuing argument. If the apostolic theologians are not part of the tradition as it actually has occurred, they will be of slight use to those currently involved. The historical-critical enterprise as usually practiced has, however, been so blinkered in its legitimate quest for, for example, "Romans' own teaching" that it has obscured the reason why the church made all these documents into one book in the first place: to guard the integrity not of many messages but of one. And indeed, leading members of the academic-exegetical guild see no reason to treat precisely these books as a unit and ignore the boundaries of the canon in their work—which is the entirely logical outcome of the viewpoint from which they see the New Testament texts.

Thus the individual theological agendas of the New Testament writers, to the discovery of which modern interpreters are likely to devote their careers, now often become the appearances that obscure what the New Testament is about. Appropriate critique is here precisely the refusal to let such appearances lead us away from the actual theological question: "How can the New Testament's theological witness now guide the church through its problem about . . . ?"

The appearances that must now be seen through emerge in large part from the volumes of brilliant historical-critical commentary that fill my shelves also. It is the creed that can and must put these very appearances "to the question," à la Bacon. A typical commentary may say, "What we learn from the story of the transfiguration is that Mark needed to illustrate Peter's confession, and shifted a resurrection story to do this." To which the creed replies, "Yes, we may indeed learn that interesting and perhaps useful fact, if it is a fact. But we must not let it obscure the theological question. What we must finally learn from narratives of the transfiguration is that when we see Jesus, as also in the Eucharist or the neighbor, we see the embodied "Glory of God.""

CHAPTER 10

Genesis 1:1–5 and the Creed

The best way to show how the creed should function as critical theory of the Scriptures will not be by further explanation but rather by providing sample attempts. In this and the following chapter, I will explicitly mention the creed more often than I might in a regular exegetical article.

I take our Old Testament text from the Bible's very beginning. There we immediately discover a disagreement about translation that is in fact a dispute about interpretation. Moreover, the dispute results from a difference between viewpoints from which the text is viewed, of the very sort to which critical theories often draw mutually disapproving attention. Should Genesis 1:1 be translated "In the beginning God created the heaven/heavens and the earth" (KJV/RSV), with "God created . . ." as a main clause? Or should it rather be translated "In the beginning when God created the heavens and the earth . . ." (NRSV), with "God created . . ." in a temporal subordinate clause?

The Hebrew does not settle the matter since the word order can at need be read either way. Nevertheless, the older translation is certainly what one would choose without some pressing reason to do otherwise; and the Septuagint unambiguously demands it. Why then do NRSV and other recent translations offer, with unimportant variations, ". . . when God created . . ."?

A mind committed to the creed as its critical guide, and suspicious of human religion, may think: these interpreters-translators have 1:2 and its parallels in the history of religions in their sights, and suppose that, in view of the parallels, the chaos described there must be antecedent to or coeval with the creating mentioned in 1:1. On this construal, the two first verses of Genesis teach that God creates by working on something, even if only a chaos, already or simultaneously present. And taken in isolation and apart from creedal critique, 1:1–2 can indeed appear to tell much the same story as was told by the myths of ancient Israel's neighborhood, in which the world-making god works by ordering preexistent chaos. Plato once summarized standard ancient mythology: "When [the Demiurge] took over the visible stuff, and found that it was not stable but was in unharmonious and disorderly motion, he brought it to order from disorder" (Plato, *Timaeus* 30A). Moreover, myth of that sort may well have provided the language of 1:2.

The NRSV's translators have thus made a possible source of the text's language determine the text's interpretation and have then translated to fit that interpretation. Why would they do that? One probable reason is that, as we have earlier noted, modern exegetes often prefer to interpret reconstructed ancestor texts instead of the texts on the canonized page; after all, making such reconstructions is much of what they are trained to do. More important, however, is that reading Genesis 1:1–2 from a certain viewpoint softens the Old Testament's challenge to humanity's normal religious predilections.

All of us, including biblical translators and the author and readers of this book, find an absolute beginning of us and our world, and a God who accomplishes such a beginning, hard to take. The gods who find a preexistent or coexistent mess and make something good of it work in much the same way as we do at our best, and so are easy to understand and deal with. A beginning to which only God is antecedent, and the God who makes such a beginning—in the language of traditional theology, who creates starting ex nihilo, "from nothing"—are harder for any of us to acknowledge. The general religious impulse, faced with the Old Testament, is so far as possible to assimilate Israel's God to the usual gods, and so in the matter of creation to assimilate him to the order-making gods that Plato summed up in his "Demiurge."

Nor is our difficulty so pristinely intellectual as we might pretend, though an absolute beginning is indeed difficult to conceptualize. If in the beginning there is something other than God, even if it is a mere chaos, and if we and our world are derived also from that something, then our existence has a source besides God, however slight or disreputable. And fallen creatures cannot but hope that we have such a foothold outside God; indeed, entertaining such a hope is much of what it means to be fallen. Even if we come to nothing or to a final horror, we at least want to claim our very own possibility of insignificance or damnation; if we are embarrassed to claim theologically déclassé works-righteousness, at least we will claim works-unrighteousness.

On the other hand, if we follow the creed's unmitigated confession of God the Creator, we will read "In the beginning God created the heavens and the earth." Therewith we will do an intellectually and spiritually tremendous thing, for there can hardly be a proposition more upsetting to our inherited metaphysical assumptions. All that side of our thinking that comes from the great Greek pagan religious thinkers is determined by a founding axiom of their thought, "Neither has any god nor any human made this cosmos, rather it always was and is and will be" (Heraclitus, frag. 30). Against such faith in the cosmos's self-founded timeless being, Christianity's doctrine of creation presents a drastically revisionary metaphysics, a construal of reality that affirms an encompassing creaturely contingency: we and all our universe might not have been. As high-medieval theology stated it with marvelous precision, no reality other than God has in *what* it is any reason *that* it is. We exist and exist as we do because God determines that we shall, and that is all there is to be said.

Our human effort to avoid Scripture's metaphysical put-down continues still. The currently standard account of the origin of our universe seems to suggest that its existence is contingent, since the universe is thought to begin with an unpredictable and inexplicable event—a "singularity"—and with wildly improbable initial conditions for development. To avoid this theologically open suggestion, some current theorists propose that our universe is but one of an indefinite multitude of universes popping up in the quantum field, ontologically antecedent to anything that might be called time. Thus reality as a whole is said not to be contingent and indeed to be timelessly eternal; by these lights, Heraclitus was in principle right. This intrinsically untestable and therefore entirely unscientific hypothesis is, sometimes explicitly, based on nothing but insistence that there be no absolute beginning, and so no role for a Creator.

Next we must ask: Who is this God who appears as Creator at the beginning of both creed and Genesis? Who is it who provides being of which no trace or potential was there before? Who is it who tolerates no antecedents, of himself *or* his works? The creed identifies him as "the Father" of the next to be introduced "Son," "Jesus Christ." Accordingly, the first article's doxology of the Father as "Almighty" and "Creator" is praise for his works, exemplified by those narrated in the article about the Son.

Therefore we may gloss Genesis 1:1: "In the beginning the Father of Jesus created the heavens and the earth." Nor is this identification without consequence. On the contrary, it even suggests that the contingency of the world is founded in the contingency of Jesus' life, death, and resurrection. It is because Jesus was truly tempted and so might have fallen, and because the Father was not compelled to raise Jesus from the death to which his steadfastness brought him, and because just this contingently faithful and rescued person is the eternal Son for whom all things were created (Col. 1:15–20) that all created being might not have been. For nearly two millennia, Christian theology has been trying, if only by fits and starts and with major backslidings, to take this metaphysically revolutionary axiom seriously; the contingently particular story of Jesus *is* the universal truth of created reality; and therefore universal truth is itself a contingent fact and not an abstract necessity.

Finally to 1:1, we must construe its relation to the following narrative of creation. Unless one is religiously committed to the notion of an independent chaos and so to the correlated interpretation of the relation between the first two verses of Genesis, the suggestion of Westermann's massive critical commentary is immediately illuminating: the verse is the *caption* of the story that follows (*Genesis*, ad loc.). If this reading of 1:1 is correct, the actual narrative of God's creating begins with 1:2, which therefore demands further attention.

Genesis 1:2, with the rest of 1:1–2:3, is generally assigned to the "Priestly" final editing of the Pentateuch. By current and plausible opinion, this editing took place well after the return from exile. We therefore must think of an advanced period in Israel's intellectual

92

history, and of a trained scholar. Did the priestly savant who fixed the final text of Genesis, laboring in some cubicle of the postexilic Second Temple, have a bit of the world's mythic understanding in him, as, given the universality of priestcraft, he might well have? Or did he instead intend to turn myth to service of an unmythic point, as do many other passages of the Old Testament (e.g., Ezek. 28:1–19)? To be sure, we do not know what his subjective intention was, and barring necromantic clairvoyance will not know, at least not in this age. What we do know is that the creed prohibits positing anything as coeternal with God. Therefore the church reads 1:2 in the second of the two ways just mentioned—as myth serving an unmythic point—and precisely as the christologically *plain* sense of the text.

Perhaps I may offer an explanation of the Old Testament's recourse to the language of myth, an explanation that is not demanded by the creed but is coherent with it. Any mention of an event, even an event like "God created," inevitably provokes a question about what came before it, since events occur within sequences. In order nevertheless to speak of an event preceded by nothing in sequence with it, Genesis appropriates the culturally available language of what we might call subsistent nothingness. Genesis, I suggest, wields the language of myth not to describe an actual state of things, but precisely to evoke creation's absoluteness as a beginning: no-thing precedes it. Chaos in Genesis is neither an actuality that God creates nor is it antecedent to creation; it marks the place of what would be other than God if he were not *Creator* of all that is other than him, and so functions to short-circuit the inevitable "But what was there before creation was there?" It is a notorious anecdote: "What was God doing before he created the world? He was making hell for people who ask foolish questions."

"And the Spirit of God was moving over the face of the waters" (RSV). Again the NRSV translates differently: ". . . while a wind from God swept over the face of the waters." Therewith the NRSV outdoes itself in remythologizing. Why would anyone suddenly translate *ruah ĕlōhîm* as "wind from God," when at its other appearances in the Old Testament it is always translated "spirit of/ from God"? To be sure, this translation is etymologically possible, and the etymology does help us to understand the actual usage. But why this reversion here? Perhaps because God's Spirit would not be present in the antecedent chaos that human religiosity wants to see in 1:2, while a wind presumably might.

93

We may gloss 1:2 in some such fashion as this: "The Holy Spirit agitated the empty possibility posited when God determines to create, but the creation is not there." How are we to understand this proposition? Perhaps as a signal that God's liveliness, his own inner identity as Spirit, puts him eternally on the brink of making something where there is nothing. Perhaps 1:2 is a hint of the possibility in God—and only in God, as one person of his triune self—that what happens in 1:3 is not impossible.

Who then is this Spirit? According to the Nicene Creed, he is "the Enlivener," *to zōopoion*; and according to the creed, what he enlivens is the church, doing so by communion with the saints, by the freedom from sin given by baptism, and by the final awakening of life in God. Moreover, since the creed locates this Spirit as the third of the identities constituting the triune name, and since the Nicene Creed even describes the Spirit's place in the triune life—he "proceeds from the Father"—they locate this enlivening of creatures as a freely chosen aim interior to God's triune life.

With all this said, and only therewith, the story of actual creation can begin. "And God said, 'Let there be light'; and there was light. And God saw that the light was good; and God separated the light from the darkness" (Gen. 1:3–4). There we have the whole doctrine in three sentences. One might think it should not take creedal guidance to discern the great points: God creates by commanding; the existence of the world is an act of obedience to his command; the initial result of his communication is an explosion of energy; this is good for something; and energy has its opposite. It turns out, however, that the one who takes all this as obvious is someone guided by the creed. For when this is not the case, the passage presents some major offenses. What do you mean "God *said* . . ."? What language does God speak? Who is God talking to, before there are verbal creatures? The other gods? How can the world be good or bad? Is not a world merely as such morally neutral? How are there earthly light and darkness before there are sun and moon? What about that story of six days, that after all starts with our passage?

How could God speak? Where monotheism of a unitarian sort, now often called "theism," has been conceptually achieved—and compared with polytheism, it is surely a considerable intellectual achievement—the God thus conceived does not speak and indeed cannot speak. Aristotle's God, which in the West is the paradigm of unitarian monotheism, does not even recognize the existence of an other than itself (e.g., Aristotle, *Metaphysics* 1072a.20ff.), never mind addressing him or her; there is a hymn to this divinity, lamentably sometimes sung even in churches, that celebrates "the silence of eternity . . ." At best, if a God like Aristotle's managed to speak, it would be a major condescension from its deity; whereas on the contrary, in Genesis "God said" is a description of the Creator's proper exercise of divine power. Or if a god of this world's religions does have someone with whom to speak, it is because he or she is one of a pantheon and is confronted and limited by other numina. Either way, the world's religion cannot conceive a God who both speaks and is *al*mighty.

On an utter contrary, a Father who has a Son that is the same one God as he is can have a true conversation within himself and so be apt to address others if he so chooses. Indeed, in the conversation he antecedently is in himself, he can issue a command to the creature that calls forth the creature's existence, to which the creature's existence is the obedient response. For the Father's eternal conversation partner, "his only Son" is himself a creature, "Jesus Christ." In John's Gospel, God's word to us is a series of conversations of the Son Jesus with the Father, which disciples are allowed to overhear (at length, John 17). And the book of Hebrews often explicitly cites Scripture as a dialogue between the Father and the Son (as in 1:1–9).

What language does the triune God then speak? He speaks the language of Spirit, the language in which the Spirit, according to the Nicene Creed, "spoke by the prophets," a universally self-translating language that the old prophets heard as Hebrew or Aramaic and the New Testament prophets as Aramaic or Greek, the language that the Spirit spoke at Pentecost to initiate "the holy universal church" and which all nations heard as their own, the multilinguistic language of the *regula fidei* in itself. God speaks the language he spoke from Sinai, the language constituted not by its surface grammar but by its role as Torah, as the communication of God's good will to his people.

Next we read that God "saw" that light is good. Does this mean that God discovers that light is good? Or is light good because God sees it that way? In general, does God will the good because it is good, or is what God wills good because he wills it? Throughout the history of theology, the matter has been argued. I myself have most often leaned to the second construal. But perhaps the most prudent judgment is that there is no humanly ascertainable difference between the two construals—and perhaps no divinely ascertainable difference either.

In any case, the real question is "Good for what?" And to this, Christian theology must answer unequivocally: good for all that is mentioned in the second and third articles of the creed. Light and its subsequent differentiation into the universe we inhabit, told in the remainder of Genesis 1:1–2:3, are there to make possible what happens with Jesus in Israel, and the sanctifying realities that accommodate its outcomes. As Karl Barth insisted with unprecedented clarity, the creation is there to provide the "outer basis," the stage and actors, for the drama of Jesus Christ in Israel. The church can recite about itself a famous passage of Jewish theology: "Israel says to God, 'It was for us that you created this world'" (2 Esd. 6:55).

The light is good. This is not said of the darkness. Does then God after all create something that is not good? Creedal critique will reject this appearance. But what then? Here is another invitation to theological proposals that need only not to be contrary to the creed.

Augustine's construction has dominated Western theology. Light, according to Genesis, is the finite being primally granted by God, and so is also the primal finite good. But light is not real except as actual shining, and in ordinary experience a finite beam of light eventually runs out. Darkness is the absence past the boundary where this happens, and thus is nothing else than this mere negation. Accordingly, evil is where being has run out, as the beam of created and so finite being eventually must. Darkness and evil as such are thus not created and indeed do not properly exist, in much the same way as chaos does not. And the evil we nevertheless experience is but the dimming of the light as it proceeds from its Giver.

Perhaps I may again offer my own proposal, which I think is not incompatible with Augustine's. Earlier I spoke of light as the first creation, which then is differentiated into the universe we inhabit, and I called the remainder of Genesis 1 the story of that differentiation. If this exegesis is permissible, the separation of darkness from light is the first differentiation, so that metaphysical darkness is the price paid for a differentiated creation.

96

Two further points are then to be made, the first rather quickly, lest longer attention precipitate us into the endless and in my opinion hopeless discussion about "theodicy," about whether God's ways with us can be morally justified. One thing can be said with some confidence: the fact of light *and* its absence, of good *and* its running out, must be inevitable in the differentiating history of a finite creation. Thus, for the perhaps central instance, continuing evolution cannot take place without death on an enormous scale.

Should then a good God have simply refrained from creating? We can no more answer that question than Job, having destroyed his friends' theodicies, could thereupon himself answer God. And it must be said plainly: the inevitability of evil in a finite creation is as good a reason as any for not believing in a good Creator, though not quite the knockdown argument presumed by some current pop atheists.

The second and quite different point. "Light" is of course Genesis's word for what we would now call "energy"; I have already presumed that identification. That the universe begins as a burst of sheer energy, that is then endlessly differentiated, is a familiar story to any who have encountered popular presentations of contemporary cosmology. Moreover, we might go on to note that the Genesis story of cosmic differentiation is followed by a narrative of chronologically successive life forms, moving from the relatively simple to the more complex—another familiar story.

One should never rest too much on agreements between "science and the Bible" since even the most firmly established structures of science are proper science only in that they remain open to being displaced. It is not Scripture whose truth we should hold lightly, but current scientific opinion, precisely on account of the latter's claim to be scientific. Thus at this writing physicists are trying to energize an unprecedently powerful particle collider; when and if it achieves full power, many usual theories of physics will hang in the balance. Still, noting perhaps temporary agreements between Genesis and scientific cosmology and biology does suggest that one historically bothersome set of appearances is illusory.

It is still said by the supposedly sophisticated and the genuinely simple, "The Bible says the world was created in six days, but science teaches that it took much longer. So much for your Bible!" And the standard answer of Christians' apologetics has for some time been, "The Bible and science are about two different things." Both parties thereby erect artificial appearances between us and what should be the obvious fact of the matter.

97

Our learned priest set out to describe the becoming of the world as God's doing, and he appropriated the best science of the day as his narrative framework—science that was, as just noted, not so far off also by current opinion. But even if the science of his day had been altogether wrongheaded, what other science might we have expected him to deploy? The science of a millennium or so after his time, which would have been gibberish for him and his readers? Or a revealed and thus timelessly satisfactory science, which just so would have been no science at all? Perhaps instead of being embarrassed by the Genesis account, we should be emboldened to emulate its courage, by similar theological appropriation and critique of current scientific opinion and problems—knowing, to be sure, that in a few centuries, if the world lasts so long, our current cosmology and evolutionary theory will seem as quaint as the tale of six days does now.

CHAPTER 11

Luke 1:26–38 and
the Creed

In the previous chapter we took a text from the Old Testament to demonstrate how the creed can be critical theory for Scripture; now we need a New Testament passage for the same purpose. Why do I choose the annunciation? In part because it is a passage that has often occupied me. But the choice can be more materially justified.

Our example should come from the Gospels, since they are the part of the New Testament where creedal critique most needs to cut through historically constructed appearances. And in the Gospels few scenes pose exegetical possibilities so theologically heavy and are so in danger of being hidden under critics' interesting but theologically irrelevant constructions, as does the annunciation.

On the one hand, few biblical scenes have through history played so large a role in the life of the church. The galleries of the great museums are filled with depictions of Gabriel's visit to Mary, made for purposes of devotion and instruction. Many late-medieval or early-Renaissance works even dictate a particular way of reading their representations of the annunciation, such as those that show a line from Gabriel's mouth to Mary's ear, perhaps with a dove moving along the line. In such depictions we see Mary hearing Gabriel's word from God, and we see the Spirit, by way of this communion, liberating Mary to be pregnant with the Word himself. Indeed, it has been said that Mary was impregnated by hearing, and so by

99

pure personal communication of the Word she would bear, apart from the intervention of any "will of the flesh."

The annunciation has been especially important for the church's understanding of itself. Through most of the church's history, telling the story of Mary and especially of her response to Gabriel was a chief way in which the church grasped its own reality. In Mary, the church has seen its archetype; what Mary is, the church is called to be. The church is called to be virginal; it is to be an exception to the passions of the flesh that otherwise rule the world. Like Mary, the church is feminine; that is, she is to be at once receptive and supremely creative. And above all, the church exists to respond to God's word as Mary did: "Let it be to me according to your word" (RSV). The shortened Latin citation that appears in many iconographic inscriptions, *Fiat mihi*, "Let it be to me," has through the centuries been a motto by which the church and its saints have grasped their own defining purpose.

On the other hand, few passages of the Gospels are so universally regarded by modern exegetes as secondary and legendary, also by many who are not in principle skeptical about the Gospels' narratives. Nor is this judgment without reason. Paul's letters, and those strata of the Gospel tradition usually regarded as the oldest, betray no knowledge of Jesus' virgin birth, much less of its announcement. Moreover, legends did quickly accumulate about Mary; a lengthy and biographically ordered collection of Mary stories, the *Protevangelium of James*, was in circulation at least by the middle of the second century, separated from the writings of Matthew and Luke by at most sixty years.

And in any case of such considerations, must not a story of human parthenogenesis, complete with an angelic messenger, necessarily be legendary? Or even if Jesus' conception was in fact virginal and somehow known by others than Mary to have been so, is not such an event of the very sort that invites legendary embellishment, whether appropriate or sheerly fabulous, as much of the *Protevangelium* plainly is?

How do we sort out history and legend? Or do some biblical stories, such as the annunciation, belong to a third category? What would that be? And supposing we judge that a biblical story is legendary, or in some other way unavailable to modernity's sort of historical investigation, how does critique that seeks to discern the triune God's agenda with the text go on from that judgment? I will

100

not take up such questions of principle at this point, but following a tendency of this whole book, I will let a proposal emerge by considering some individual items of our passage.

"The angel Gabriel was sent by God." An "angel," from the Greek *angelos*, is a messenger. In our passage, this function is explicit: God has sent Gabriel with his word for a maiden of Nazareth. And as on every occasion when the Word of God is sent out, it "does not return empty" (Isa. 55:11); the maiden in fact conceives.

This particular angel's role in God's creation is not, however, limited to messenger service. In Luke's parallel story of an annunciation to John the Baptist's future father, Gabriel is again a messenger but further describes himself as one who stands "in the presence of God" (1:19). With that we are in the milieu of, for example, the opening scene of the book of Job, where "the sons of God" (RSV, KJV) or "heavenly beings" (NRSV) gather to "present themselves before the LORD"—seemingly as something like a heavenly officialdom, since one of them initiates the following drama by reporting on his portfolio as investigating officer for human affairs (1:6–7). The standard construal, which I accept, is that where such beings appear in the Old Testament, or are carried over into the New, they are depotentiated deities, the gods of the polytheism amid which Israel lived, demoted by Israel's faith to be servants of the unique and jealous God. Creedal critique will only insist that this was their true status all along, that whatever their ontology may otherwise be, if they exist at all, they were and are creatures like the rest of us and in no way divine or semidivine.

What sort of reality are we then to assign to heavenly entities other than human saints, if they are not even semidivine? The church's thinking cannot simply deny their existence. The Nicene Creed amplifies the first-article praise of God as Creator of "heaven and earth" with the antignostic "and of all things visible and invisible"; and whatever else the creed may embrace in "things . . . invisible," the "angels and archangels" of many eucharistic prayers are certainly included. Thus a creedal critique of our passage cannot be simply skeptical about Gabriel but rather must seek to discern his role in God's agenda with the texts in which he appears, and to conceptualize his reality accordingly—perhaps, to be sure, in less mythic terms than here (for possibilities, see Jenson, *Theology*, 2:117–27).

101

Here what we must see through is our culturally erected supposition that because the story of the annunciation is of another genre than those with which modernity's historical research can deal, nothing like what it narrates can "really" have happened. And indeed, once the creed has made us stop to think, it may occur to us that the supposition is anyway not very plausible, unless we have so crudely idealist a notion of history as to suppose that only what we could in principle know can have happened. On the obvious contrary, there must be vastly more of reality that is intrinsically hidden from our research than is available to it.

Unlike most of Scripture's heavenly beings, our angel has a personal name; he is identified by this name in the two Lukan annunciation stories and, most informatively, at Daniel 8:1–26. The passage in Daniel is an early example of the style of prophecy we label "apocalyptic"; for a full-fledged sample of the genre, we may conveniently look to the New Testament's own apocalypse, the book of Revelation (chaps. 4–22). Prophets like the John of Revelation see a vision in which heaven opens to reveal what is in it (4:1). What is seen in heaven is God enthroned and ruling, and "what must take place after this," that is, the present and future course of God's rule, displayed in stylized figural or ritual drama. The genre is literary: the seer is to record what he has seen in order to report it to readers, the John who receives the Revelation has pen in hand. From the time of the Babylonian exile to shortly after the time of Jesus, the writing of apocalypses became a dominant form of prophecy in Judaism and then in the church.

Thus Gabriel's ontological location is as a dramatis persona of such visionary drama; and since the vision is given to the prophet in order to reveal the reality of God's history with his creation, Gabriel cannot be classified simply as fiction. If the story of Gabriel's visit to Mary is not available to confirmation by historical research, it transcends such history not in the way of legend but in the way of apocalyptic prophecy's vision of history's underlying agenda.

Gabriel is sent "to a virgin," *pros parthenon*, named Mary, who despite her virginity "will conceive . . . and bear a son" (Luke 1:27–31). It will be best first to dispose of the linguistics, about which some modern exegesis has made unnecessary difficulty. The reference to a prophecy in Isaiah is indeed unmistakable: "A young woman shall conceive and bear a son" (7:14 RSV). The Hebrew for the prospective mother is *almâ*: lexically, a sexually mature young woman. Thus a pregnant *almâ* may be either virginal or not, unlikely as the former eventuality may appear from certain view-

102

points. Much modern commentary's unreflected supposition that Isaiah's pregnant young woman must of course be pregnant in the usual way is an exegetical *petitio principii* that betrays a particular and—creedal critical theory will judge—inappropriate viewpoint. Moreover, what is often not emphasized is that the Greek Septuagint is unambiguous, reading *parthenon*, which must be translated "virgin"; therefore we may at least say that neither Gabriel nor Luke is guilty of an exegetical error, since for much of Second-Temple Judaism, and thereupon for Luke and the ancient church, the Greek Septuagint was the functionally canonical text of the Tanakh/Old Testament.

In any case of such linguistic possibilities, according to the creed Jesus was born of "the virgin Mary." The church's exegesis will therefore leave "virgin" in its Lukan place.

But what exactly does calling pregnant Mary a virgin entail? Whatever it may or may not suggest about her later postpartum gynecological state, it at least forbids male participation in the conception of her child. Why would the creed, which leaves so much out, demonstratively follow Luke in this one matter? What big difference is Joseph's exclusion from Jesus' biological lineage supposed to make?

It is regularly said that the primary import of the creed's "born of the virgin Mary" is that Jesus indeed had a mother who can be named, as at the other bracket of mortal life he had an executioner who can be named. Both phrases enforce Jesus' humanity; he truly was born of a particular woman, and he truly died at particular human hands. This is undoubtedly correct so far it goes, but it does not explain why the name "Mary" is not sufficient by itself, as "Pontius Pilate" is. If it is advanced that "virgin" early became an expected honorific epithet, like one of the invariable Homeric epithets, this is no doubt true; but in the *Iliad* "tamer of horses" regularly goes with "Hector" because in the story Hector actually is a notable tamer of horses.

Again I propose a theory not demanded by the creed, but coherent with it. Suppose Joseph had been Jesus' father: the incarnation would then have taken place by "the will of" Joseph's "flesh," whereas those who are "of God" are not born "of the flesh" (John 1:13). For however we construe the roles of male and female, one difference is plain: male flesh cannot in the event of conception embody a pure *fiat mihi* to God's word, as Mary's female flesh

103

could. Male flesh will or will not rouse itself as *it* wills. If we, who have fathers and so exist by the will of a piece of flesh, are nevertheless by union with Christ to be of God and not of the flesh, Christ cannot in this matter be in the same status as are we.

It could be and has been objected that someone with no father according to the flesh would not have the same "human nature" as we, so that our union with him would again be blocked, only now from the other side. But the Spirit, who within the triune God's one work of creation is the Liberator from what we must perceive as impossibilities, can bestow human nature—whatever that actually is—as he wills.

So did "the virgin birth" happen? We have no theologically neutral way to answer yes or no; and indeed, claims of theological neutrality about questions of this sort are usually cover for some quite particular theological commitment.

In this case, the intruding commitment is one that we moderns are all too likely to harbor. We have become accustomed to thinking of events like the virgin birth as "miracles," as exceptions to known laws that otherwise govern the world's behavior. Yet we should note that this concept of "miracle" never appears in the New Testament, where the word usually translated "miracles" is *dynameis*, events simply requiring uniquely enabled agents. We have become accustomed to regarding modern science's warrants and results as constituting an encompassing system of truth, within which such unexpected claims as a virginal conception must be accommodated. This ranking indeed puts such claims in a precarious epistemic position: when we look at reality in this fashion, a story about a virgin conception—or about the stilling of a storm or the opening of atrophied eyes—indeed becomes an offense to reason.

But what if our presumptions have it backward? What if the story warranted by the regularities and connections available to modernity's scientific investigation should not be inflated into a "metanarrative," the only one that modernity will tolerate? What if they do not provide the universal explanation of which modernity dreamed? What if Mary's virginal pregnancy is in order and unproblematic, even predictable, within a universal narrative authored by the Creator, within, that is, the one true metanarrative? What if in that narrative Mary's virginal pregnancy is warranted by laws both more encompassing and liberating than the "laws of nature"? It is precisely such a godly universal narrative that is dramatized in apocalyptic vision, in which narrative Gabriel and virginal Mary are agents and the story of annunciation is an incident.

It is perhaps time for Judaism and the church to say out loud: the story told by modern cosmology and biology is an abstraction from the truly encompassing story of reality. It is an abstraction that is splendid and fascinating within its own scope, and is amazingly powerful for immediate practical purposes. But for critique that penetrates to the apocalyptic depth of reality, and to the connections and ordered sequences that there determine events, expectation that the Word's human conception must occur without male contribution may be nothing more than a judgment of sound probabilistic reason. As Thomas Aquinas more broadly put it, "If we judge with respect to God and his power, there are no miracles" (*Summa* 1.105.8). I will take up this theme again in the concluding Afterword.

We have not yet arrived at the chief burden of Gabriel's message: that Mary's son will occupy the throne of David (Luke 1:32). Apocalyptic prophecy is still prophecy; here Mary is the prophet, and Gabriel communicates the promise she is to bring, to Elizabeth and to those who will read.

Indeed, Mary may be seen as the archprophet, who brings forth the Word in person, addressed to all people and all times, as other prophets brought forth the Word in partial texts and discourses, addressed to particular historical situations. It is perhaps first and foremost in this role that she should be seen as archetype of the church, of the community that claims to fulfill Joel's promise that all God's people will prophesy (Joel 2:29–30), a community that indeed is called to be a single communal prophet, and to be just so a true image of Mary.

Historical-exegetical questions again threaten to interpose themselves where they do not belong, to become in fact appearances needing critical dispersal. Was the Judaism of Jesus' time indeed as animated by hope for a Christ as traditional Christian apologetics have supposed? If it was, were one or many Messiahs expected? And of what sort? Did Jesus regard himself as the Messiah? It would be interesting and in some contexts important to have answers to these and other such questions, but here again interpreters have so pursued such information as to hide the place of Gabriel's promise in God's agenda. The creed directs us so to read the Old Testament and the Gospels as to perceive that the God of Israel indeed has a "Son," and that this Son is Jesus "the Christ." As to what the Christ is to do and accomplish, the creed's second article tells some of his doings and the third article some of what he accomplishes.

The last sentences of the previous paragraph do not restrict what a teacher or preacher may adduce in naming the promised blessings of the Messiah, also in interpreting our present text. On the contrary, the creedal articles open the whole of both Testaments to their christological plain sense. In expounding Gabriel's promise that Mary's child will be the Messiah, the homiletical or catechetical interpreter may profitably trace the whole history of the promise to Abraham, as it intensifies and expands through God's blessings and judgments in history, and through the Word that comes to the prophets, until it is fulfilled as Christ rises "in accordance with the Scriptures." The interpreter may reflect on the "holy catholic church" as the community of the Christ, or on baptism as incorporation into him, or on the final triumph when his reign and the Father's are one. Indeed, as the event is perceived from the creed's viewpoint, what the annunciation announces is the whole of God's work.

And finally we must attend to one particular aspect of what is promised to and then by Mary: her son will be called "holy, . . . the Son of God," *huios theou* (Luke 1:35). How are we to read this? At first, we may read it as a messianic title. But does not the fact that the Messiah can be so designated have further theological import? In the creed, this title appears in a sequence with the "Father" title of the first article and the "Holy Spirit" of the third. Moreover, it acquires the modifier "only," stipulating that Jesus' filial relation to the Father is ontologically unique. All that is to say that the creed makes the Son be one of the Trinity, so that "Son of God" can even be reversed to be "God the Son," *theos ho huios*.

Gabriel announces to Mary that her son will be God the Son. This makes her the mother of God. But obvious though the logic is, theologians have often tried to avoid it. Can God really be born of a woman? A man who somehow may be called God the Son, yes; but God the Son himself? It may be noted that the church's actual misogynists have generally been the heretics: thus those who in the fifth century denied that God could have a mother were openly moved by sheer disgust at the notion that God could have inhabited that musky place, a woman's womb.

No less a personage than a patriarch of Constantinople, Nestorius, tried to root out his congregation's penchant for praise of Mary as Theotokos, "Mother of God," thereby provoking the christological controversy that led to the Council of Chalcedon in 451. The council ruled that "one and the same" Son was born in eternity of the Father, and in time was born of Mary. And most Christians therefore beg her intercession with these or similar words: "Holy Mary, Mother of God, pray for us sinners now and at hour of our death."

CHAPTER 12

Mark 14:35–36
and Dogma

To test the efficacy of postcreedal dogma as critical theory for biblical exegesis, we again pick a central text. The scene is the Garden of Gethsemane, where Jesus' arrest is imminent. (A version of some parts of the following exegesis of this text appeared in Davis & Hays, *Art.*) Like the annunciation, Gethsemane has through the history of the church been painted, sculpted, and sung.

Mark reports that Jesus "threw himself on the ground and prayed that, if it were possible, the hour might pass from him." Then Mark continues, "He said, 'Abba, Father, for you all things are possible; remove this cup from me; yet not what I will, but what you will'" (NRSV/RSV). According to Mark and Matthew, Jesus uttered the prayer three times. This scene will be our test case of dogma as critical theory of Scripture.

We should, with RSV and KJV, translate "Not what I will, but what you will"; NRSV's "want" is not demanded by the Greek—though in some contexts it is allowed—and attributes wants to God, who has none. Or so at least the creed, with "almighty," tells us. God indeed has genuine purposes, goals that in his own sort of time—called "eternity"—are future to his present, but not because he is in any way wanting; precisely his goals constitute his eternal plenitude.

The prayer is a famous crux of the exegetes. And it cannot be ignored, since it appears in all three Synoptic Gospels and is probably alluded to also by John. We will abide by the scholarly consensus and presume that Mark is the source for Matthew and Luke—and perhaps in this case, if in backhanded fashion, for John as well. A striking feature of Mark's text already poses the exegetes' problem.

Mark begins by setting the scene in Gethsemane and in doing so mentions the prayer by quoting it indirectly. Here Mark has "if it were possible" and thus makes Jesus' rescue depend on a possibility that may not obtain. But the immediately following direct quotation of the prayer has Jesus assert that all things, including his rescue, are possible. Which is it? It will not do to say that Jesus was first uncertain and then certain of the possibilities, since we do not have citation of two prayers but indirect and direct quotation of the same prayer.

Could Jesus have been spared? Or indeed, since escape is explicitly labeled "what I will," could Jesus have followed this will of his own and chosen to evade the coming horror, perhaps going back to Galilee or seeking reconciliation with the authorities? What exactly is or is not possible here? And for whom is something possible or not possible?

The vexation of the exegetes began already with Matthew and Luke, both of whom edited Mark to reduce occasion for such questions—or so we may plausibly surmise by noting what they omit. Matthew suppresses "All things are possible," and unlike Mark provides a direct citation of the prayer's second iteration, where he has ". . . if this cannot pass . . . ," more strongly suggesting that rescue may not be possible (Matt. 26:39, 42). Luke takes more drastic action and altogether removes the language of possibility. As for John, he flatly disowns the prayer, quoting Jesus as proclaiming: "What should I say? 'Father, save me from this hour'? No, it is for this reason that I have come to this hour" (John 12:27).

Possibility, necessity, and will are the parameters of all narrative. Thus the antinomies just noted put at risk the narrative integrity of both the scene in Gethsemane and, as we will see, the general Gospel narrative.

Could Jesus have followed his own will, evidently different from the will of the Father? If we come to the text simply with creedal doctrine in mind, we are likely to say that since Jesus is himself God the Son, this was not possible. But this answer ruins the Gethsemane story, turning the prayer and anguish into pretense.

What the passage plainly describes is a choice being made then and there by Jesus, to accede to his Father's will, a choice that determines the course of events.

If, on the other hand, we are unbothered by doctrine about Jesus' deity, or suppose we can bracket it out methodologically, we are free to say what at first seems obvious: the story presupposes that Jesus could have chosen his will over the Father's. But this reading also ruins the story. For the Gethsemane scene has its drama only as part of the total gospel narrative; and in all the Gospels this narrative is shaped by a constant sense that Jesus' life is governed by divine necessity, and that this necessity is internal to his own personhood. "Was it not necessary that the Messiah should suffer these things and then enter into his glory?" (Luke 24:26).

Indeed, it seems that the only answer that preserves the narrative integrity both of the scene itself and of the Gospel narrative in which it is an incident is that Jesus could have fled and that if this had occurred, this too would have belonged to the divine necessity that moved his life. But where does that leave us theologically?

Next we must note that the creed provides little or no direct help with this dilemma. At least, nobody perceived any help before seventh-century dogma came to the creed's assistance. The fathers of the ancient church, when obliged to interpret our scene, regularly punted, even though they were fully armed with the rule of faith or the creed. They often could think of nothing better than to construe the prayer and anguish as—not to put too fine a point on it—pretense: Jesus himself was surely not really tempted to back out, but he behaved as if he were, to provide believers with a model of prayerful submission in time of trial.

We can cast the puzzle in other terms. Mark's report describes and then narrates one side of a conversation. Between whom? One side is identified: the words are addressed to Jesus' "Father" and are specified as prayer. But who speaks these words? Who says, "Remove this cup from me; yet, not what I will, but what you will"? Obviously, the man Jesus says them, but if we follow the dogma decreed by the Council of Chalcedon, this only sets the problem.

According to Chalcedon, the subject of all action and suffering in the Gospels' narrative is a single person, who is truly God the Son and truly the human Jesus of Nazareth; insofar the council fathers followed Nestorius's nemesis, Cyril of Alexandria. This doctrine excludes a solution that may at first seem attractive, that it must have been simply the man Jesus who can have prayed in such fashion as to distinguish his will from the Father's will. No, says Chalcedon, when Jesus prays, God the Son prays.

But if then the Son's personal will is active here, and if we assume that God the Son wills at one with his Father, this makes God the Son will one thing and the man Jesus another, so that there are two wills in one act of one person. What sense can that make?

Dogma again prevents us from resolving this last question in a way that may first come to mind: we cannot adduce the psychological phenomenon of "being of two minds." A psychological interpretation of Christology had already been tried and found wanting: in the fourth century, the considerable theologian Apollinaris of Laodicea, a friend of Athanasius, proposed that the Son united himself with the man Jesus by inhabiting him as the root of his psychology, the spirit in a three-part anthropology of body, soul, and spirit. But the Council of Constantinople in 381 decreed that this would not do. Whatever may be the components of human nature, they are also in Christ's case human components. There is no empty slot in his humanity for his divine will to occupy.

The alternative is that God the Son and the man Jesus speak as one voice and say to God the Father, "Not what I will, but what you will." But is a possible divergence of wills between God the Father and God the Son thinkable? We seem again to be at a standstill.

Despite patristic theologians' continuing best efforts to avoid these questions, they slowly became irrepressible. It was an omission by the Council of Chalcedon that opened the path of serious controversy. The council accomplished a great deal. It decreed that "one and the same" person is the single protagonist of the Gospel narrative, the worker of salvation. And it adopted what has remained the standard, though now sometimes questioned, christological terminology: there is one "hypostasis"—one identity—of the incarnate Son, who has two "natures." He shares divine nature with the Father and the Spirit, and human nature with all of Adam's descendants. But while Chalcedon's decrees wax eloquent about the inviolable integrity of the "two natures," they have nothing equivalent to say about the ontological status or integrity of the "one hypostasis."

112

Followers of Cyril of Alexandria, suspicious of lurking "Nestorianism," decided that this silence about the ontological status of the Savior's single personhood was no accident. And they rightly supposed that much was at stake, for in Scripture it is indeed not a divine nature or a human nature or even the two in cooperation that do the works of salvation, but the single protagonist of the one Gospel story. In the interests of full disclosure, I should say that I am wholly on the side of the Cyrilleans.

Dispute between the more determined followers of Cyril and Chalcedonian loyalists shortly hardened into schism. Many anti-Chalcedonians reverted to what had once been Cyril's preferred formula, "There is one nature of the Logos, that has become flesh," and came to be known as "monophysites," "one-nature-ites." To this day there are monophysite churches in old territories of the Eastern church, most notably Egypt's Coptic church and the Armenian church, though the latter sometimes disclaims the label.

Through the sixth and seventh centuries, theologians of the Chalcedonian state church made various efforts to win back the monophysites, moved both by genuine theological concern and by alarm about the fragile unity of the empire, threatened by the religious alienation of important populations. Finally, in the seventh century, they rather desperately took to devising dogmatic formulas specifically tailored to accommodate the monophysites. They could not agree to "one nature" without abandoning Chalcedon altogether, but they needed something with "one," *mon-*, in it. They first proposed that in Christ there is but "one action"; the proposal was "monergistic." At least in retrospect, this actually seems appropriate, but some Chalcedonians would not accept it, thereby deepening the monophysites' suspicions. Next the imperial theologians proposed that in Christ there is but "one will."

This monothelitic (one-will) proposal sparked the last christological controversy of the ancient church—unless we suppose that the later iconoclastic controversy was basically christological—and provoked one of the last great intellectuals of the ancient world, pagan or Christian, Maximus the Confessor, to strenuous thought. Maximus is notorious for subtle distinctions and argument, cryptic dicta, and nearly impenetrable Greek diction. I will not here try to sketch his thinking in its own terms and will rather report what I can make of it.

It is natural for God to will, in whatever way we can say such things about God, and it is also natural for humans to will; thus will belongs both to Christ's divine nature and to his human nature.

113

Therefore the monothelitic proposal will not do. Maximus immediately saw this and supported a dyothelitic position: if Christ has two natures, divine and human, he must have two wills, divine and human. But how can that be? We seem to be back at the beginning of our problem.

The following is how—I think—Maximus worked this out. The two natures of Christ are not in the same way related to the others who share those natures. The man Jesus is an individual who instantiates human nature, just as do all individual descendants of "the Adam." Therewith he instantiates the human capacity of willing. But Father, Son, and Spirit are not in that way instantiating individuals: that would make three gods. Indeed, the divine nature is not *instantiated* at all, but obtains only as the mutual life of Father, Son, and Spirit. Therefore, since in the hypostasis/natures scheme will belongs to nature, the divine will does not belong to Father, Son, or Spirit as a capacity of any of the three, but occurs only in their mutual life. Thus the Son's divine will is not his individual possession; it occurs as his role in the triune willing.

Maximus therefore could say that the man Jesus makes a human decision, with all that inheres in a genuine human decision, and that this is the only *individual* decision made at Gethsemane. And he could then propose that since Jesus and the Son are but one hypostasis, Jesus' act of human decision is itself the Son's participation in the mutual triune deciding that is the divine will, here that Jesus should suffer. Jesus makes a human decision, and this decision is present in the divine life, as the Son's part in a triune act of willing. And since this triune event *is* the divine will, it is this that belongs to the Son's divine nature.

A third Council of Constantinople, in 681, rejected monothelitism and defined dyothelitism, "two-will-ism," as the true doctrine. It is doubtful that the council fathers knew or could have followed Maximus's reasoning; the council's own explanations are not wrong, but they leave the problem mostly where it was. Since dyothelitism is incoherent without Maximus's analysis or something like it, we are justified in taking the council's decision as permission for us to work out the matter more or less as Maximus did.

Returning to our text to read it by the light of such dogma, we may say that the man Jesus' human decision to obey the divine will is the *content* of the triune decision, as we may perhaps further say that the Father's monarchy is its finality and the Spirit's freedom its

114

integrity as decision. We see in Gethsemane a man making a hard decision, and may believe that this human event takes place in the triune life, in which it is decided that this man will be faithful.

Could Jesus have fled? No, because his life is governed by the triune will, here by the triune decision that he will be faithful. Yes, because his human decision not to flee constitutes, in its specific way, that triune deciding. Both the "all things are possible" and the "if it were possible" are true. The preacher should say: "See your hope in God at stake in this man's struggle, and rejoice in its glorious outcome."

Finally in this chapter, we must note the difference between creed and dogma, as critical theory for reading Scripture. Dogma, such as that of Chalcedon or Constantinople III, is not like creed immediately founded in the church's initial communal consciousness. To know that proposed dogma is in fact dogma, we must identify it as enabled by the Spirit's continuing guidance of the church's magisterium. But how do we know when this is the case? How do we know that the church's magisterium, wherever we locate it, has in fact spoken? Since not every proposal that seemed formally in order has proved out? We have no other recourse at this point than to recur again to creed and canon. Therefore when we do the sort of thing I have done in this chapter, we are not only being led by dogma to God's intent for a passage of Scripture; we are also, vice versa, reconfirming the validity of the particular dogma in play, by testing its efficacy as a guide to scriptural understanding and as a logical corollary to the creed.

Afterword

I could perhaps think of yet more "extensions," but that, I fear, would be stretching our defining concern rather too far. And if I were asked to say anything more on the central matters, I fear I would merely repeat myself in other language. Therefore, instead of pursuing either of these paths, I will as a final word try to put the whole discussion into an, in my judgment, needed larger frame. For not all true propositions of theology are creedal or dogmatic, and biblical studies encompass many more methods, problems, and generally accepted results than I have adduced.

This may also be the place to acknowledge the obvious, that the historical reach of my discussion has been mostly limited to the ancient Mediterranean church and the Western church, which inherits its achievements and problems. Including discussion of the role and problem of canon and creed in the ancient church east of the Euphrates or in Orthodoxy or in the flourishing modern African and Asian churches would have been beyond both the practicalities of an essay and the knowledge of the author—and repair of the latter would have delayed publication by several years.

The foregoing chapters are, each in its own way, at once description of how creed and canon work together—or in some few matters do not work together as well as they might—and a plea for the church to recognize their mutuality and its vital role in its life. For the sake of its integrity through history, the church must always remember that canon needs creed and creed needs canon, and that it is permitted to govern its discourse and practice by their joint import. The church would hardly have survived immersion in the religious and moral farrago of late Mediterranean antiquity, or confrontation with the political and intellectual challenges of the medieval period, without the mutual admonition of canon and creed—or perhaps something called church would have survived but would not have been the church of the apostles. And those parts of the modern Western ecumene most afflicted by modernity's alienation between and from creed and canon are unlikely to remain even nominally Christian beyond the present generation unless they quickly learn again to rely on the aid they have been granted.

To be sure, even believing that the church has in fact made it this far, that there is now an actual church to worry about, means trusting in the Spirit's past action to preserve the church in spite of itself, in large part by the instrumentalities of canon and creed. That same faith is our only ground for hope that the Spirit will also now bring us through, again in part by these instruments and despite our bewilderment in their presence.

But now to that broader context. The necessary mutuality of canon and creed is one aspect of a necessary unity of the study of Scripture and theology generally. And the current alienation between canon and creed is but one part of a separation between theology and biblical scholarship that has developed through several centuries.

Before modernity, what we are now likely to call systematic—or dogmatic or constructive—theology was not thought of as an enterprise distinct from biblical exegesis. Indeed, such foundational masterworks as Thomas Aquinas's *Summa theologica* or Origen's *First Principles*—with which Origen created the whole discipline of systematic theology—were written as preparatory studies for what their authors regarded as the real theological work, reading Scripture with understanding. Prospective students of Scripture needed to know what were the historically bothersome problems in understanding the biblical message, as the creed revealed that message, and what answers the church had adopted to many of these. Particular theologians' proposed solutions for other such problems were then simply part of an ongoing work at that task.

In modernity, it has been just the other way around; we have supposed that biblical scholarship must come first, with theology coming thereafter to make what it can of the biblical scholars' results. The very curricula of the seminaries and surviving theological faculties are organized around the assumption that biblical scholarship on the one hand provides the materials for theology, and on the other hand does not itself presuppose theological learning or disciplined theological reflection. The curriculum instructs us to ask first, "What did texts from the various parts of the Bible mean in 'their own terms,' 'back then'?" Only thereafter are we to ask, "Whatever are we now to do with all these witnesses?" We do not notice that presumptions hidden in the way the first question is cast make the second question unanswerable.

What lies behind this reversal? How did we come to think that biblical exegesis is to provide raw materials for theology? Materials that regularly prove recalcitrant or indeed unusable? How did theology come so regularly to be practiced either as a sheerly speculative discipline, or as rehearsal and application of doctrine supported only by the authority of the church or believers' experience?

It was a founding maxim of modernity: "Only the metaphysical makes us blessed, never the historical." In modernity, only what is true always and for everyone, and is in principle available to everyone, was acknowledged as the sort of truth that sustains human life. The burden of human well-being cannot, it was proclaimed, be carried by "truths of history," which are particular and contingent, and just so knowable only as they are carried to us by traditions whose beginnings and paths are themselves contingent and neither reach all humankind nor are universally affirmed by those they do reach. Only an odd dissenter or two thought to ask if indeed there are any both universal and universally acknowledgeable truths, or suggest that if there are any such generalities, they might just so not be salvific—or even very interesting.

It is time and past time for the church to say without hedging that modernity had it backward. Few would want to eschew modernity's many material and political blessings, but the way in which modernity related truth and tradition is now manifest as the great error that it was, and indeed as a culturally and even demographically suicidal error; alienated from their Christian tradition, the culturally European peoples have lost the will even to reproduce themselves. In increasingly manifest fact, the well-being of actual humanity in its several communities is established and preserved *only* by tradition, and so by the particular and contingent events that traditions mediate.

It may be too late for Western civilization to be rescued from itself. Nietzsche's detailed and accurate narrative of its decadence, *Thus Spoke Zarathustra*, was after all published in the 1880s. But the church is not permitted to despair of the civilization it cocreated until the death has been certified; meanwhile, we must doggedly keep on criticizing and proposing. And whether any attempt to rescue Western culture succeeds or fails, modernity's reversal must surely be reversed in the thinking of the church itself.

We must summon the audacity to say that modernity's scientific/metaphysical metanarrative—at the moment told by astrophysicists and neo-Darwinians—is not the encompassing story within which all other accounts of reality must establish their places, or be discredited by failing to find one. It is instead a rather brutal abstraction from reality. The abstraction has proved to be magnificent in its intellectual power and practical benefits. Nevertheless, by these disciplines' methodological eschewal of teleology, they prevent themselves from describing what actually is. As pop scientists urge over and over, the tale told by Scripture and creed finds no comfortable place within modernity's metanarrative. It is time for the church simply to reply: this is certainly the case, and the reason it is the case is that the tale told by Scripture is too comprehensive to find place within so drastically curtailed a version of the facts. Indeed, the gospel story cannot fit within *any* other would-be metanarrative because it is itself the only true metanarrative—or it is altogether false.

By current standards the claim just stated surely is preposterous, but if the gospel is true, it cannot be withdrawn or mitigated. For not only does God own the gospel history as his own, he is himself a character within it; he is both the Father of the Christ and himself the Christ. How should such a narrative find space within some other? Those who own the triune God must maintain the claim: all other aspiring accounts of reality have their truth, if any, within the biblical story of Christ's coming.

120   Those who own no God are perhaps condemned to continue stretching science's devices and results to make them seem universally explanatory. But the effort becomes ever more desperate.

Thus it was recently loudly proclaimed, "There is a specific region of the brain that becomes active during 'religious' experience!" Yes—well—what would you expect? What would, for instance, a Thomist theologian expect, who construes the soul as the Aristotelian form of the body? And in any case, what exactly about religion does this banality explain?

Theology and biblical exegesis cannot be restored to their ordained harmony so long as also the church's thinking presumes modernity's divorce of universal truth and tradition, and subsequent pitting of the first against the second. The first condition of theology's and exegesis's renewed mutual integrity is overcoming this error, at least within theologians' and biblical scholars' own working suppositions.

This does not mean that we should or can simply repristinate premodern theologoumena that coordinated universal truth and tradition, under such rubrics as "nature and grace" or "reason and revelation." Mere repristinations of past intellectual structures are always a dubious enterprise. And our present opportunity, with the experience of modernity behind us, is to do *better* than the premoderns. The way is open for the church's thinking to be at once more concentrated on the particular person of Christ and more clearly universal in its scope than it has ever before managed to be; indeed, theology must and can be each *because* it is the other, and must be able to say why this is so.

What the theology and biblical scholarship of the next decades must accomplish is a single flow of what modernity's theology separated as dogmatic reflection, exegesis, and speculation. All modes of churchly reflection should be braided like the branches of an alluvial stream, with the branches mutually disposed as the momentary flow of discourse suggests. If this study of creed and canon can contribute in any slight measure to the emergence of such thinking in the church, it will have been worth the effort both of readers and the author.

BIBLIOGRAPHY

Most listed classic works that have standard interior reference systems and are used in the text are listed by English titles and without edition or version.

For Further Reading

Gaventa, Beverly Roberts, and Richard B. Hays, eds. *Seeking the Identity of Jesus.* Grand Rapids: Wm. B. Eerdmans Publishing Co., 2008.

Hanson, R. P. C. *The Search for the Christian Doctrine of God.* Edinburgh: T&T Clark, 1988.

Harnack, Adolf von. *Marcion: The Gospel of the Alien God.* Translated by John Steely and Lyle Bierma. Durham: Labyrinth, 1990.

Hays, Richard B. "Reading the Bible with Eyes of Faith: The Practice of Theological Exegesis." *Journal of Theological Interpretation* 1 (2007): 5–21.

Jonas, Hans. *Gnosis und Spätantiker Geist.* Göttingen: Vandenhoeck & Ruprecht, 1934.

Luther, Martin. *Commentary on Genesis.*

Works Cited or Explicitly Referenced

Allert, Craig. *A High View of Scripture?* Grand Rapids: Baker Academic, 2007.

Aristotle. *Metaphysics.*

Bauckham, Richard. *The Testimony of the Beloved Disciple.* Grand Rapids: Baker Academic, 2007.

Byassee, Jason. *Praise Seeking Understanding.* Grand Rapids: Wm. B. Eerdmans Publishing Co., 2007.

Campenhausen, Hans von. *Die Entstehung der christlichen Bibel.* Tübingen: Mohr, 1968.

Cullmann, Oscar. *The Earliest Christian Confessions.* London: Lutterworth, 1949.

Davis, Ellen F., and Richard B. Hays, eds. *The Art of Reading Scripture*. Grand Rapids: Wm. B. Eerdmans Publishing Co., 2003.

Eichrodt, Walther. *Ezekiel*. Philadelphia: The Westminster Press, 1970.

2 Esdras = *4 Ezra*.

Gregory the Great. *Homilies on Ezekiel*.

Hahneman, G. M. *The Muratorian Fragment and the Development of the Canon*. Oxford: Clarendon, 1992.

Harnack, Adolf von. *Die Entstehung des Neuen Testaments*. Leipzig: Hinrichs, 1914.

Heraclitus. *Fragments*.

Irenaeus. *Against Heresies*.

Jenson, Robert W. *Systematic Theology*. 2 vols. New York: Oxford University Press, 1997–99.

———. *Unbaptized God*. Minneapolis: Fortress, 1992.

Jeremias, Joachim. *The Parables of Jesus*. New York: Scribner, 1955.

Justin Martyr. *Dialogue with Trypho*.

Kelly, J. N. D. *Early Christian Creeds*. New York: McKay, 1972.

Levey, Samson H. *The Targum of Ezekiel*. Collegeville, MN: Liturgical Press, 1990.

Lips, Hermann von. *Glaube, Gemeinde, Amt*. Göttingen: Vandenhoeck & Ruprecht, 1979.

Nietzsche, Friedrich. *Thus Spoke Zarathustra*.

Origen. *First Principles*.

Plato. *Timaeus*.

Protevangelium of James.

Schaff, Philip. *The Creeds of Christendom*. New York: Harper, 1931.

Soulen, R. Kendall. *The God of Israel and Christian Theology*. Minneapolis: Fortress, 1996.

Thoma, Clemens. *A Christian Theology of Israel*. New York: Paulist Press, 1980.

Thomas Aquinas. *Summa theologica*.

Trobisch, David. *The First Edition of the New Testament*. New York: Oxford University Press, 2000.

Westermann, Claus. *Genesis*. 3 vols. Neukirchen-Vluyn: Neukirchener Verlag des Erziehungsvereins, 1966–82.

Young, Frances. *The Making of the Creeds*. London: SCM Press, 2002.

SCRIPTURE INDEX

125

SUBJECT INDEX